PENGUIN BOOKS

A MINNESOTA BOOK OF DAYS
(AND A FEW NIGHTS)

Howard Mohr lives with his wife and daughter on
five acres of southwestern Minnesota prairie. For
recreation he likes to tinker with old cars or scan
the horizon with binoculars. As a longtime writer
for "A Prairie Home Companion," Howard Mohr
created more than two hundred scripts and spots,
including "Raw Bits," "Worst Case Scenario,"
"One-Minute Romances," "Pentagon Overstocks,"
and "The College of Lo-Technology." He fre-
quently appeared on the show in his own material
as Howie Humde (owner of the Walleye Phone
Company), Herb (of Herb's AcuAuto, the Midwest's
only acupuncture garage), Bob Humde (inventor of
the CowPie Key Hider), and as a Minnesota voice
in the ads for "Minnesota Language Systems," the
simple cassette tape and study guide that became
the heart of Howard's *How to Talk Minnesotan*.

10/4/95

Dear Connie,

Someday you'll forgive
me for bringing you to
Minnesota. Maybe it
will be after you read
this! (Maybe not)

Love, Polly

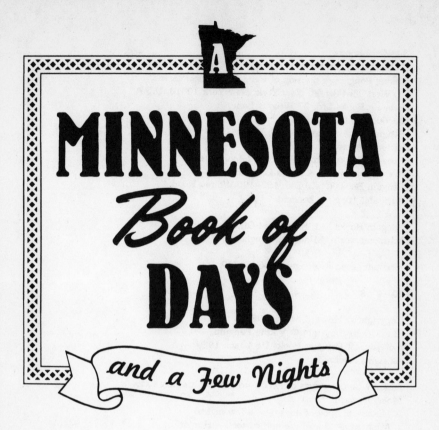

A MINNESOTA Book of DAYS

and a Few Nights

Howard Mohr

PENGUIN BOOKS

PENGUIN BOOKS
Published by the Penguin Group
Viking Penguin, a division of Penguin Books USA Inc.,
40 West 23rd Street, New York, New York 10010, U.S.A.
Penguin Books Ltd, 27 Wrights Lane,
London W8 5TZ, England
Penguin Books Australia Ltd, Ringwood,
Victoria, Australia
Penguin Books Canada Ltd, 2801 John Street,
Markham, Ontario, Canada L3R 1B4
Penguin Books (N.Z.) Ltd, 182–190 Wairau Road,
Auckland 10, New Zealand

Penguin Books Ltd, Registered Offices:
Harmondsworth, Middlesex, England

First published in Penguin Books 1989

10 9 8 7 6 5 4 3 2 1

LIBRARY OF CONGRESS CATALOGING IN PUBLICATION DATA
Mohr, Howard.
A Minnesota book of days (and a few nights)
1. Minnesota—Social life and customs—Humor.
2. American wit and humor.   I. Title.
PN6231.M57M6 1989 818'.5402   89–8619
ISBN 0 14 01.1833 0

Printed in the United States of America
Set in Bookman
Designed by Fritz Metsch
Illustrations by Warren Sattler

To Jody:
I hope the second
thirty years together don't
go by so fast.

FOREWORD

By Harold Mire

The guy who put me in this book told me I could say whatever I wanted to here and he wouldn't touch it. I find that hard to believe. He's so used to making stuff up for a living, I don't see how he could keep his hands off the Foreword. A good example of his breezy attitude toward the truth is the way he disposed of my '70 Chrysler Newport. I bought it used in 1979 from a Lutheran pastor who obviously had a habit of driving with his foot in the carburetor between visits to the sick and shut-ins: it had 67,000 hard miles on it when I began nursing it toward 139,000, which is when I discovered the rusted main frame and decided to retire it.

Now my friend the author had me take the hood and trunk lid off the Chrysler and fill the whole thing with black dirt to make a planter and mini-greenhouse. What really happened is, after I stripped it of radio, headlights, and other useful objects, including the engine and seats, I used my old Ferguson tractor/loader to push the Chrysler deep into the grove behind the house. Ethel was in charge of steering it. I had put a lawn chair on the driver's side so she'd have a place to sit. I'll never forget the for-better-or-worse look on her face as she rocked and lurched into the trees, but she did a good job of parking it between the rusty binder and the remnants of the windmill tower that got twisted in a tornado in 1958. If I stood up right now at the east window of the kitchen, I could see the tail end of the Chrysler. It's comforting to know it's there. Mice live in it and every so often one of our cats will get inside through the rusted wheel wells and do some hunting.

It's not a federal crime, making things up, but I just don't want somebody dropping by our place and expecting tulips and carrots growing out of the Chrysler.

The author has been a friend of mine for a long time, and his family, too. If I wrote a book with him in it, I'd probably start with the night his cat, Sugarsweet, appeared in the moonlight under the bedroom window in summer and meowed his name. She woke him up and kept meowing until he went to the back door and stepped outside in his underwear. When he looked into the cat's eyes he was sure that the soul of a dead person he had loved had taken possession of her. He said that's when he realized that where he lived on the prairies of Minnesota was home for good and he himself would haunt that house and building site when he died. It's a true story about him, and I'm surprised he didn't make it happen to me and put it in this book.

JANUARY

1

THIS NEW YEAR'S MORNING IN 1985 HAROLD AND
Ethel Mire woke up almost simultaneously at 4:15, even though
they had nearly made it to midnight on New Year's Eve playing
cribbage.

Harold woke up first, after doing one of his midair acrobatic
turns from his left side to his right side, the result of a dream about
water-skiing on sand through a reptile park. The impact of his
touchdown on the bed's rigid surface flipped Ethel over onto her
face and brought her immediately to a full-alert status.

It was the old problem: should they get up now or should they
try to sleep one hour and forty-five minutes more until the alarm
went off at 6:00? They elected by voice mumbles to go for more
sleep, but at 5:59 they scrapped the project when the alarm clock
made the tiny click that meant it was winding up to strike.

They realized then that they should have got up at 4:15 and
had breakfast and been that much further ahead on the day, but
now they were so tired from having concentrated so hard on getting
back to sleep, they could barely drag themselves out of bed. It
colored the whole day.

That night they were tempted to hit the hay early to make up
the sleep deficit, but that would just make them wake up earlier
than ever tomorrow. So they sat in a stupor from 9:00 until 10:30
P.M. with not even enough energy to watch the weather news, let
alone comprehend its complexities.

* * * * * * * * * * *

2

THE BELLTON CENTENNIAL CELEBRATION WASN'T
until July 10, 1989, but the beautification process had begun early
on this winter day in 1988. There were two sides to the issue.

The Committee for Beautification's position was simple:

Many of the people who had left Bellton in the last few decades
would be returning for the Centennial, and why not let them see
Bellton at its beautiful best—with new siding on the liquor store
for instance. And take down those dumb champagne-bubble lights

that don't blink anymore. The Committee issued a directive to those residents on the west edge of town, where the hordes of visitors would be streaming in on State 45: do some painting and get those junk cars out of your yards and cut the weeds once. In fact they issued several directives to several people over the weeks to come.

The Coalition to Oppose Beautification also had a simple position: they refused to be pushed around by a bunch of hypocrites. The town had been okay for ninety-nine years and now they were supposed to slap on some cheap cosmetics and pretend they were something they were not? Besides, it was their opinion that the people who left had good reasons to do it, the prime reason being they probably had their fill of Bellton's solid citizens trying to make them march with a goose step.

The Committee for Beautification held this private view: they wanted Bellton to look so good that the people who left would feel bad they had abandoned such a charming and progressive town.

The Coalition to Oppose Beautification said that most of the visitors would be coming back to see the town as it was—including the tractor dump on the north edge, the Sigertson barn that had been sitting in a slump since 1943, the boarded-up window of the hardware store. All the sights. It would be a big disappointment if the deserters drove hundreds of miles to Bellton and it looked like the set for a Hitchcock movie where horror was just below the slicked-up surface. Besides, it stuck in the Coalition's craw that the Committee for B. would go to all that trouble for people who didn't live here anymore.

Because of this conflict, two parades were eventually planned, two historical pageants, and come hell or high water, the four square blocks west of the Lutheran church would not be touched by Beautification. Guards would be placed around the clock to keep it the way it was.

*   *   *   *   *   *   *   *   *

3 MINNESOTA BIGFOOT WAS SIGHTED PICKING OUT A new refrigerator at a Sears store in Minneapolis today in 1986. He seemed definitely to want the No-Frost feature, but he did not want both the ice dispenser and the cold-water tap in the door, because he could put the ice in a glass and then fill it at the sink.

The salesman could see him wavering and said, "My experience is that you should always get more refrigerator than you think you need, because a couple of years down the pike you'll wish you had."

* * * * * * * * * * *

4

This day in Minnesota is sponsored by THE ACKBOM FAMILY PLATE COLLECTION:

*An exclusive offering of Myron & Martha Ackbom
*Each plate is a full nine inches in diameter
*None of that bleed-through or blurring found on
    cheaper plates
*You'll kick yourself if you don't get in on it

MYRON SEZ:
Our friends always tell us we have the best vacation slides they have ever seen and it's not just because we serve such good snacks when they come over. And that got Martha and me thinking that maybe the general public would like to own a few of our outstanding shots after they'd been memorialized on the eating surface of a limited edition of ACKBOM FAMILY PLATES. What we did, we put a second mortgage on the house to bankroll our dream, and Martha and I moved all the junk out of the garage and started firing the first beautifully crafted plate in the Ackbom collection.

The premier ACKBOM FAMILY PLATE features a picture I took at a rest area on Interstate 90 in South Dakota during our summer trip in '78. I know it wasn't '79, because we still had the '73 Chevy, which you can just see the damaged left fender of on the corner of the limited-edition plate where some bozo backed into it in the Red Owl parking lot and took off. In '79 I traded up to a '76 Ford even though I had been a Chevy man all my life. It's been a good little car for us, but now I'm at the stage where I've got to grind the valves or trade her. It's a tough call.

The camper van at the top of the first ACKBOM FAMILY PLATE belongs to a retired bus driver and his wife from Fargo. They were in the back of the camper taking a nap when I shot the picture.

That's Martha at the picnic table getting our lunch set up. You can see our dog Bummer in the background. He's tied up in the pet exercise area, God rest his soul. Just before Groundhog Day in 1981, Bummer was accidentally compacted by the garbageman and hauled to the landfill. Teddy's reading comics at the end of the picnic table and his sister is in the bathroom getting some paper towels for us.

Won't you help us preserve part of the Ackbom family heritage for generations to come? Enclose $45 in cash for each copy of "Rest Stop." (Sorry, only two dozen per customer, please.) Send your money to:

> Ackbom Family Plates
> c/o Myron Ackbom
> Route 3
> Boxelder, Minnesota

You'll receive your first ACKBOM FAMILY SLIDE PLATE just as soon as we can get it wrapped in newspapers and stuffed in the box. Each plate will have a number and a certificate of authenticity stuck to it, and will include the complete details about where and when the slide was taken. I've only touched the surface here. And don't worry about your investment being compromised, either. When we reach our production limit on each attractive plate, we'll run over the stencil with the lawn mower.

If you like our first issue, great—then we'll automatically send you the other nine plates as we manufacture them. I'll be on the second plate by myself, except for the gigantic muskie I'm holding by the gills. I played it in on eighteen-pound-test monofilament line in '79 or '80. You'll get the whole story with the plate.

If for any reason you are not satisfied with "Rest Stop," it's yours to keep, but don't ask for a refund. It would be like a slap in the face to us.

This is a one-time deal. If you don't order by the end of the month, you'll never again have the opportunity to accept our plates. Myron Ackbom doesn't make idle threats.

* * * * * * * * * * *

5 ON THIS DAY IN 1988 HAROLD MIRE WENT TO SEE the family doctor and told him that he'd been a little worried lately about death, his in particular, but not exclusively, and he felt like a Class-A loser, and then there was the fairly gloomy realization that civilization was on the skids, that nobody took pride in work anymore, that it was basically a dog-eat-dog world with not much of a future for the kids, and a guy might as well move to the desert and live in a cave.

"Go fishing, Harold."

The prospect of spending a day on a frozen lake inside a dark icehouse with a bag of sandwiches made Harold sleep so well, the next day he got up and decided to stay home and saw wood. He was a tough cookie when it came to recreation.

*   *   *   *   *   *   *   *   *   *

6 IT'S NOT TOO EARLY TO DECIDE ON A HIGH-SCHOOL prom theme today. The Land of Oz is a good choice, but the flowered arch is overpriced and the yellow brick crepe won't hold up. And don't expect the football boys to dress like Munchkins either. Maybe you should go with Night of Memories: the stars hanging from the gym rafters could be used next year. Stars are always good to have around.

*   *   *   *   *   *   *   *   *   *

7 ON THIS DAY IN 1958 THE FIRST DOMESTIC TRASH compactor was invented. The critics said that there was no way you could get the American public to buy and install in their kitchen a noisy, expensive machine whose sole purpose was to crush garbage into a huge block that the kids couldn't carry out and you couldn't dig through without a crowbar and gas mask if you remembered you lost your wedding ring while fixing supper.

*   *   *   *   *   *   *   *   *   *

8

TODAY COULD BE THE DAY YOU FINALLY LEARN HOW to rip off and shake open one of those thin plastic supermarket bags in the vegetable section without hurting yourself or attracting a crowd.

* * * * * * * * * *

9

EARLY ON THIS WINTER DAY IN 1988 HAROLD MIRE took the occasion of his forty-ninth birthday to start his autobiography in a house on the frozen prairies of western Minnesota where he had lived with Ethel for twenty years. Tentative title: *Me.* Reprinted by permission.

> *It is I, gentle reader, an American male with dry, flaky scalp and crumbs of toast stuck to his pajama top. I was looking out the kitchen window just now and what I saw was dirty snow, piles of it. And I asked myself some big questions. Am I the first forty-nine-year-old man to stand in his sock feet covered with dust bunnies and wonder how he pissed away nearly half a century? Would medicated shampoo work? How come I'm so tired when I get up no matter how long I sleep? Should I consider the sparrows in the lilac bushes above the drifts, how they toil not neither do they spin? Then I remembered it was lilies.*

* * * * * * * * * *

10

HAROLD MIRE CONTINUED HIS AUTOBIOGRAPHY ON this day in 1988. New title: *Diary of a Dope.*

> *I slept late today and in that dark REM period between first waking and waking up later I dreamt of the time my '55 Chevy ran out of oil on the Kansas freeway and I kept going*

*because there was no place to stop and the rod bearings were
thumping . . . and then the thumping was my heart and I was
wired up to a machine that monitors the past. My life was
printing out on a graph. It was a flat line with tiny burps on it.
The doctor was a beautiful woman. I can see my name at the
top of the graph: Mr. Rube. She speaks in hushed tones to her
colleague, a young man dressed in his medical degrees. Then
I hear one clear sentence:* If this guy was going to make it there
should have been some sign of it by now.

*   *   *   *   *   *   *   *   *   *

11

HAROLD MIRE WROTE ANOTHER PARAGRAPH IN HIS
autobiography on this day in 1988. The new title: *Boy, I Don't
Know.*

> *I could tell you anything. There's so much to tell and yet
> so little. And some of it I don't recall very well. If I hop around,
> pardon me. I never did get a date with Sharon R., who every-
> body said was the county queen of heavy petting when I was
> in high school in Fremson in the mid-'50s. I think Sharon was
> in 4-H and had Grand Champion sheep four years in a row.
> But I could be confusing her with this other girl, Becky, who
> had a nose like a light bulb. Becky did raise sheep, I know,
> and always wore wool jumpers. Sharon was also in Future
> Homemakers of America.*

*   *   *   *   *   *   *   *   *   *

12

HAROLD MIRE CHANGED THE TITLE OF HIS AUTO-
biography to *Yeah, I Suppose* on this day in 1988 and wrenched
another paragraph out of his soul:

> *How the whole thing got started beats me. Kids were saying
> that Sharon and I went to a Dean Martin/Jerry Lewis movie at
> the Orpheum on our date and then parked in front of her house
> and steamed up the windows of my family's '42 Plymouth coupe*

for three hours. But that wasn't me. It was a kid named Doug Parsnip who attended school at Lobel, about ten miles north on Trunk Highway 15. And they didn't go to a movie. They went straight to the quarry and took an air mattress out of the trunk of a Chevy with a hot Olds engine in it. At least that's the way Doug told it every chance he got.

*   *   *   *   *   *   *   *   *   *

13

MINOR LEAGUE WAS THE NEW TITLE OF HAROLD Mire's autobiography on this day in 1988 and his head was hurting when he wrote now:

> *The fact is, I never did date any heavy petters in high school. I bought a bag of coconut cookies once at the FHA Spring Bazaar that were baked by Sharon though. They were doughy. The girls I went out with had good penmanship and when we got home their mothers would start flipping the porch-light switch, which was a great relief. First base to me in those days was a cloth-covered bag ninety feet from home plate that I tripped over if I ever got a hit.*

*   *   *   *   *   *   *   *   *   *

14

THE HAROLD MIRE AUTOBIOGRAPHY WAS CALLED *Keeping My Hair in Place* on this day in 1988:

> *My brand of hair fixative until I was a junior in high school was H-A, Hair Arranger. It was green with chunks of congealed oil in it. It made my pillow translucent. When I discovered Vaseline as a hair dressing, my high, sweeping front wave stayed put all day. It wouldn't even move in a strong wind. Another advantage of Vaseline was it made the collars on my shirts water-repellent. A disadvantage was that my forehead and ears were always shiny. Girls paid more attention to me, though. They would dare each other to go by me in the hall and touch my wave.*

*   *   *   *   *   *   *   *   *   *

15

TODAY IN 1988 HAROLD MIRE'S AUTOBIOGRAPHY
took a turn he didn't like one bit and ended abruptly after the
following agonizing entry. Harold allowed it to be reprinted with
the rest because he said it would be a good lesson to people who
thought they wanted to scrape up the past for fun and profit. New
title and last: *Who Needs This Crap?*

*Oh, I forgot about my second date with Marie. The first
date was almost in the fun range and ended in the obligatory
trip to Flip's Drive-in for a tenderloin. The Flip's tenderloin in
those days was a slab of pork that had been hammered, breaded,
deep-fat fried, and thrown on an oversized bun. It was probably
suggestive food to most of the kids.*

*When I picked Marie up at her house for our second date,
her mother was glaring through the parted curtains. We were
headed for the Minnesota State Fair, three hours away. At noon
I was beginning to think this might be the beginning of something big. But by mid-afternoon we were sitting on a grassy hill
overlooking the Family Pavilion—no, that's not right: she was
sitting, I was slumped. My face must've been the color of
putty—I had seen it in the mirror when I felt this sick before.
My forehead was sweating, and I was swallowing like crazy.
Then I noticed the plop of mustard on my left shoe and I had
to make a dizzying run to the toilets. That was all she wrote on
romance.*

*The rest of the day is a blur. When I got home that night
my mother said, "Did you have a good time?"*

The eternal question.

And the eternal answer: Yes.

*Goodbye, readers. And good riddance, if you don't mind my
saying so. I'm going back to car repairs and wood sawing and
manure scooping.*

*   *   *   *   *   *   *   *   *   *

16

SCANDAL ERUPTED ON THIS DAY IN 1988 WHEN A picture of Prairie Gate College President M. Rolf Peterson's $9,000 desk appeared in the Mortwood newspaper. State Representative Robert Dobbins pretty much expressed his constituents' feeling when he said, "It's not the money so much as it is the bad taste involved here on the part of President Peterson. That $9,000 desk looks to me like a $200 autopsy table." President Peterson apologized for his poor judgment and gave the Prairie Gate Board of Trustees a personal check for $9,000 and gave the desk to his brother-in-law, who later sold it for $17.50. President Peterson restored confidence in his administration by having the Prairie Gate College Physical Plant build him a new desk out of a telephone-cable spool.

*   *   *   *   *   *   *   *   *   *

17

ON THIS DAY IN 1970 THE FRONT DOOR SOCIETY was organized by a group of radical farm women from western Minnesota. Their goal was to get people to use the front door of their farmhouses instead of the back door that comes in through the kitchen and goes by the basement stairs and usually has two or three huge jumbles of overshoes and brooms and overalls and you name it. And what kind of impression does that make? The big question was: What's a front door for anyway!!!? What's the point of remodeling the house and putting on this front porch, and an entryway with coat closet, and this beautiful big heavy door with scrollwork, if nobody uses it except for wedding receptions and graduation lunches? And what's that sidewalk for in the front if not for walking on to get to the front door?

The Front Door Society's first tactic was lobbying the legislature for passage of a law that would have forced people, under threat of punishment, to use other people's front doors and not just drive up and knock on the back door, which doesn't even have a nice lighted doorbell button. But mainly they developed a program of education which involved the distribution of literature to rural boxholders and visits to the schools. Their original guidelines were hardnosed:

1. Put up a strong gate across the driveway that leads around to the back of the house.
2. Install PARK HERE and ENTER THE FRONT DOOR signs out front on the lawn.
3. Put a blinking neon-light arrow on the front door.
4. Allow your immediate family to use the back door only if their feet are muddy or they are heading for the basement shower to wash off herbicide or manure.

By 1974 the Front Door Society, in an act of desperation, began suggesting that farm women could get a carpenter out and have him switch the doors around, and make the back door look like the front door and the front door look like the back door. It worked, only too well. Everybody came in the front door and tracked mud across the living-room carpet and the kitchen in order to get to where they wanted to be in the first place, which was the stairs to the basement inside the back door, no matter what it looked like from the outside.

That was the straw that broke the Front Door Society's back. They reorganized as the Dining Room Society, whose single purpose was to get people to eat in the dining room instead of hanging around the kitchen all the time. What's a dining table for anyway, to pile stuff on?

*   *   *   *   *   *   *   *   *

18 ON THIS DAY IN 1988 HAROLD MIRE WENT TO THE Medical Park for the second time in two weeks. A popping squeak had developed in his elbow. It was no big deal during the day, but at night it woke him up when he moved it.

"It sounds like a distant gunshot," Harold told the guy sitting next to him looking at country kitchens in a *Modern Home.*

"Well, if they can't fix it here you can always go to the Mayo Clinic. Billy Graham goes there they say."

Dr. Sheromes, the Mire family doctor, listened to Harold's

elbow through a stethoscope and said: "You know, it sounds like a distant gunshot."

"I could've told you that on the phone. I came here for the big cure."

"It's been a long tough winter so far, Harold—what you need to do is shovel snow lefthanded until spring comes. Give that squeaker a rest."

"That's it?"

"Unless you elect to have surgery. What I'd do is install a grease zerk on your elbow so you could lubricate the joint before you went out to scoop."

*   *   *   *   *   *   *   *   *   *

19

THE NEW PRIMATE WING OPENED AT THE MINNESOTA Zoo on this day in 1988. Three stockbrokers captured in New York were housed behind one-way windows and allowed to invest millions of dollars of what they thought was real money belonging to real people. Record crowds were entertained by their bad decisions until February, when the primates were moved to a permanent home in San Diego.

*   *   *   *   *   *   *   *   *   *

20

MINNESOTA BIGFOOT WENT TO THE TICKET COUNTER at the Minneapolis/St. Paul International Airport on this day in 1988 to use his frequent-flyer credit for a free trip to Orlando and was told that there were no seats available on that flight for participants in the program. After Bigfoot jumped up and down a few times and beat on his chest, several seats opened up, including the one he was given in First Class. During the flight he was served two trays of hors d'oeuvres and a special thirty-ounce rib-eye steak dinner with three bottles of Heineken Dark.

*   *   *   *   *   *   *   *   *   *

21 ON THIS DAY IN 1948 KYLE BEEKEN INTRODUCED A household product he hoped would put him on easy street. He called it "Anti-Shock Sheet." It was basically a perfumed square of chemically treated paper you were meant to toss into your automatic clothes-dryer in order to "stop static cling," he told the gathered reporter.

The critics were merciless—they said there was no way you would ever get the public to buy a harebrained product like that. But what mainly sank Kyle was that very few people had automatic clothes-dryers in 1948 and those who did had no idea what static cling was, because the synthetic fabrics that caused fully dressed people to turn into electrical-generating plants, and bedclothes to snap and crackle in the dark, hadn't been fully foisted on consumers yet.

* * *   *   * *   *   * *   *

22 ALONG TOWARD SUNDOWN ON THIS DAY IN 1986 Harold Mire took a snow shovel out behind the house next to the grove and dug himself a cave in one of the eight-foot drifts. After the ten o'clock news, Harold told Lily and Ethel that he was planning to sleep outside inside a snowbank.

"Why?" Ethel said.

"What if I got lost in a blizzard sometime?"

"I get it," Ethel said. "It's a test, like the time you laid on your back in the dark in the cellar crawl space under the bathroom to see if you could do it in case you ever had to."

"A guy has to be prepared. Anything can happen."

"It's already zero out. I suppose there's nothing I can say that will stop you?"

"I don't think so."

"Well, I'll see you in the morning then," Ethel said.

"If you're lucky," Harold said.

Lily didn't say a word. She went upstairs and wrote another letter to Ann Landers, but she didn't mail it because one of her parents was still borderline normal. Besides her friends would know who wrote it right away even if she used a fake name and state.

* * * * * * * * * *

23

IN 1984 IN MINNESOTA A TOTAL OF 37.5 MAN- AND woman-hours on the average every day, including this one, were spent peeling the inside top seal off a new jar of instant coffee after punching a hole in it to hear the tiny inhalation of air into the vacuum-packed granules. One and two-tenths person-hours were spent wondering why only instant coffee had this sort of sealing arrangement. Of the active seal removers not one was able to grip the seal at the edge and peel it off in one piece. Some people did not spend any more time removing the ragged remnants of the seal on the jar's edge, but of course two person-hours were wasted every day thereafter trying to thread the lid on straight.

A hardcore minority of instant-coffee aficionados over sixty years old did not remove the complete seal; they carefully used a paring knife to make a half-moon-shaped entry hole a teaspoon would just fit through, the idea being that the coffee would stay fresher that way (not supported by scientific evidence) and that the straight edge of the entry hole would automatically create a standard of measure by scraping the excess from the spoon.

* * * * * * * * * *

24

ON THIS DAY IN 1987 ERWIN BURDOUX RECEIVED in the mail his official Exclusive-TopDog catalog from Gopher Liquidators. The range of goods and the incredibly low prices made him dizzy. How could they do it and make money? And he got the leap on those chumps that didn't have the sense to pay $60 to get the TopDog inside scoop and reap additional savings and not ever have to suffer because something was sold out forever.

Erwin immediately called the Valued-Customer toll-free number and placed an order with Nancy on his credit card: she seemed to sense that he was somebody special when he took a set of three

Rhino Lamps at BELOW DEALER COST!!!! He would've been a fool
not to get them. But Erwin really won Nancy's admiration by getting himself a stylish executive chair for $19.50 when the poor man-
ufacturer's suggested retail price was $487. Nancy said they would
be shipping his items within five days—more special treatment.

* * * * * * * * * *

25

ERWIN BURDOUX CALLED GOPHER LIQUIDATORS
this day in 1987 and asked for Nancy. "Nancy. It's me, Erwin.
Remember? Executive chair?" She sounded tired, but she perked
up after Erwin ordered the tiny TV set and pulse monitor that
fitted on his wrist for $39 when it originally sold for $300. And
then he took a motorized rotary snack-dip set for $32 that the
Gopher Liquidators catalog said you couldn't touch anyplace else
for less than $150. Erwin could see the quality in the photo. "The
thing is, Nancy, Babs and I are planning to do more entertaining."

* * * * * * * * * *

26

WHEN ERWIN BURDOUX CALLED TO PLACE HIS
order today in 1987 at Gopher Liquidators, with selections from
his Exclusive TopDog catalog, Gloria said that Nancy was ill and
Erwin said to give her his best. He'd call tomorrow.

* * * * * * * * * *

27

ERWIN GOT ON THE PHONE EARLY TODAY IN 1987.
"Nancy, glad you're feeling better. I won't talk long, but I do need
a couple of those Exer-Jock arm builders on page seven, and why
don't you keep the gold necklace on page nineteen for yourself and
put it on my card. I hope you'll compare it at $120 when you wear
it, Nancy."

* * * * * * * * * *

28 ERWIN BURDOUX ALMOST TOOK THIS DAY OFF IN 1987 from calling Gopher Liquidators, but he really felt he needed to snap up the phone-answering machine with the massage attachment on page 45 of the TopDog catalog before they were all sold. He also ordered the rechargeable fish scaler and head remover at below dealer's cost.

*   *   *   *   *   *   *   *   *   *

29 ERWIN BURDOUX WAS DIALING THE LAST DIGITS OF the toll-free TopDog order number when Babs came back early from a trip downtown for a new dress. She told Erwin she had never been so embarrassed in her life. The clerk at Bowzer Boutique put the credit card in the machine and the alarm went off for being over the credit limit and they held her arms and took the card and snipped it in two right in front of six customers. They told her she was lucky they didn't call the police. "You haven't bought anything on it lately, have you?" Babs said. Erwin said, "Well, a couple of things we needed around the house."

Erwin would miss talking to Nancy and he guessed he'd have to do without the gasoline-powered mulcher that he could use to make humus in the garden if they ever moved out of the apartment and bought some land.

*   *   *   *   *   *   *   *   *   *

30 ON THIS DAY IN 1988 HAROLD MIRE HEARD TWO different people say that if you stood long enough in Times Square, everybody you knew would walk by. Harold figured that if he was crazy enough to stand in Times Square, it wouldn't be five minutes until he would see the professional educator who gave that two-hour commencement speech at the Mortwood high school last year. Times Square was right up his alley. And Ethel's old college room-

mate, she'd go by twice before the day was over. But no matter
how long he stood in Times Square, Harold knew one person who
would never walk by, and that was his Uncle Henry. In fact you
could stand in Las Vegas, or The Epcot Center, or even Knott's
Berry Farm and never see Uncle Henry walk by. If you wanted
to see Henry walk by, you'd have to stay closer to home, his home.

*   *   *   *   *   *   *   *   *   *

31

SELF-SERVICE GAS-STATION STATISTICS RECENTLY
compiled for Minnesota reveal that on any given day—this one
for instance—customers will remove the nozzle from the hook on
the pump and an average of three ounces of gasoline that's always
left in the nozzle will either splash on the customer's shoes or be
lost on the ground. Figures indicate that all the gasoline spilled in
this way in a single day would be enough to carry by bus all the
self-service gas-station attendants in Minneapolis to Disney World
for a week.

The amount of gas lost at self-service stations when the automatic shutoff doesn't work on the nozzle and the gas splatters on
the sleeve of your coat and runs down the side of the car would
be enough for every customer to drive a few blocks to John's, who
has been filling 'er up for forty years and does the windshield and
talks about the weather and actually knows the way to the place
you want to get to and gladly tells you. He also knows what that
thing with the three wires sticking out of it under the hood is and
can fix it.

John is the guy who should get the free trip to Disney World
and let those other guys continue to petrify on the stool behind the
cash register.

*   *   *   *   *   *   *   *   *   *

END OF JANUARY

31

END OF JANUARY

FEBRUARY

1

THE ANNUAL STATE CABIN-FEVER SUPPORT-GROUP rally convenes on this day in the Humphrey Metrodome. Blizzard date: February 20. Second backup blizzard date: February 27.

* * * * * * * * * *

2

ON THIS DAY IN 1987 THE MACRO 10-4, THE world's first vegetarian truck stop, officially opened on I-35 south of Burnsville, serving bottled water, soyburgers, tofu chops, herbal teas, rice cakes, dessert without white sugar, and other healthful and sometimes attractive foods.

The first customer was Dorton Buldey, hauling plumbing fixtures out of Kansas City. After a brief ceremony of welcome performed by the staff, in which bird feathers were placed in a circle and a small ode was read, Dorton asked for "a cheeseburger, fries, black coffee, and a big piece of that coconut-cream pie" and was told by the waitress, Teri, to consult the menu and besides that was not pie in the refrigerator case, it was yogurt soufflé with bee pollen.

Dorton decided on a bean-sprout open-face sandwich on triticale bread, with a side of goat cheese. He washed it down with a cup of Afternoon of the Faun tea. Dorton could taste it all the way to Bemidji.

Teri and the cook were meditating when the second customer pulled his rig in, so he left. The third customer thought it looked closed.

* * * * * * * * * *

3

DRIVING A TANKER OF CORN SYRUP TO FARGO ON this day in 1987, Larue Samuel almost became the MACRO 10-4's fourth customer, but before he ordered, he touched Teri on the shoulder and said, "My, you are a cute one." Teri dialed 911 and made a citizen's arrest.

*   *   *   *   *   *   *   *   *   *

4 THE MACRO 10-4 STAFF DECIDED ON THIS THIRD day of business that education was the problem and began handing out position papers to the potential customers, explaining the MACRO 10-4's nutritional philosophy and listing the major poisonous foods found on supermarket shelves.

*   *   *   *   *   *   *   *   *   *

5 THE MANAGEMENT HAVING CHANGED OVERNIGHT and also some of the decorations, the MACRO 10-4 became Donny's Cafe at the dawning of this day in 1987. By sunset Donny's had served 127 beef commercial plates, twenty-five loaves of white bread, and thirty gallons of coffee that had a kick like a mule. The eleven pies in the case looked like homemade banana creme until about 3:00 in the afternoon, when there was nothing to see except a smear of whipped cream on the glass. Donny had also dropped 140 pounds of frozen french fries into boiling fat between 11:00 in the morning and midnight of his premiere day.

*   *   *   *   *   *   *   *   *   *

6 This day brought to you by MINNESOTA CHURCH BASEMENT RESTAURANTS OF NEW YORK.

If you live in the Big Apple, you've got to be fed up with high-priced restaurants that rotate you and their undercooked food at the top of a tower. You're ready to walk down one flight to a MINNESOTA CHURCH BASEMENT RESTAURANT, featuring folding chairs, banquet tables covered with butcher paper, and friendly Minnesotans serving you the finest in Minnesota-style cuisine in a church-basement setting.

*No reservations—go on in and make yourself at home.

*Don't ask for a quiet table for two near a window. There aren't any windows. But don't worry, they've got fans.

*Each table seats thirty and serving begins when it is filled.

*Overhead fluorescent lights create a warm atmosphere that melts the ice.

*Drape your coat over the back of the chair.

*No tipping.

*The maître d' has been replaced by the food caller, who announces each food item over the PA system.

*The largest all-you-can-eat dessert selection in the Northern Hemisphere: lemon pie, strawberry pie, apple pie, pumpkin pie, chocolate sheet cake, mint dazzler, coconut-Velveeta bars, cherrybomb bars, killer fudge bars, Blarney Stone bars, hope-chest carrot bars, and the no-bake one-pound butter bars.

*Tuck in the napkin, fasten your seatbelt, load your plate, pass the bowls to the left, and get to know the people around you.

If you're a Minnesotan with a strong desire to serve and are willing to relocate, why not get in on the basement floor with a MINNESOTA CHURCH BASEMENT franchise in the Big Apple. Also looking for Minnesota moms and grandmas to cook and decorate. It's a wide-open field where you'll be cooking with gas.

*   *   *   *   *   *   *   *   *

7

YOUR FIRST SEED CATALOG MAY HAVE ARRIVED IN December, but by this time in February, if you are a serious gardener—or simply a comic gardener—you should be receiving one or two seed catalogs a week in the mailbox. In the hard winter months of January and February in Minnesota and the weaker winter months of March and April, thumbing through seed catalogs is like visiting Lourdes. What can it hurt?

Miracles can happen, as Malcolm Finders, of Blinking Eye, Minnesota, began finding out on this day in 1983, as he reached page seven of his new *North Country Seed* catalog. It had been one of two items in his mailbox: the other was a flyer from a company that sold gabardine pants with cuffs to large men. There it was, a face he never dreamed he would lay eyes on again: it was Jim Thornton, his old roommate from the university in 1957, smaller than life, holding in his left hand a hybrid White Burpless cuke that had apparently made him happy. Malcolm had played darts with Jimbo for a penny a point and a dime a game when he should have been preparing himself for the multiple-choice test in Western Civilization. Jimbo dropped out and moved to San Francisco to be a beatnik and never wrote. He hadn't gained any weight since college, or he lost it, which was more than Malcolm could claim. The rest of *North Country Seed* had happy strangers in it.

*   *   *   *   *   *   *   *   *   *

8

ON THE VERY NEXT DAY IN 1983 MALCOLM FINDERS found the Blinking Eye *Journal* in his mailbox with a headline announcing that a new filter system would be purchased for the sewage-treatment plant. Under the paper was the *New World Garden* catalog. And on page 18, there she was, Patty Hearst. The word balloon at the side of her head said Patty thought the Giant Purple Radish was the tastiest radish she had ever sunk her teeth into; they averaged fifteen pounds and weren't woody. You could slice pieces off all winter. She was smiling. Malcolm thought it looked like a good deal in a radish, and besides he had always thought that photo of her in a bank with a machine gun was retouched by somebody who didn't like her.

*   *   *   *   *   *   *   *   *   *

9

ON THIS DAY IN 1983 THE *OLDTIMER SEED AND Nursery* catalog was the lone occupant of Malcolm Finders' mailbox. On page 4 was Nixon, Richard M. Nixon, living past President. Take your pick he said. He seemed to speak right out to Malcolm about how he wanted to embrace all the varieties of tomatoes on his page: the low-acid, the cherry, the Glacial Ridge. He loved tomatoes more than anything else that grew on earth. Tomatoes were the center of his world. And in Nixon's hand, held out like a TV evangelist's Bible, was a perfect specimen of the Big Guy Boom-Boom, ten seeds for a dollar, one order to a customer. Mr. Nixon promised that it would produce large juicy fruits until the first snowfall. It was good for canning, good for the table, good for the market, good for what ailed you. Nixon was grinning again, relaxed, content. Malcolm was glad to see that the grim days of his troubled presidency were behind him now even though he was still wearing the same blue suit. And the dog that was peeking out from behind the huge vine—no, surely not—didn't he die?

*   *   *   *   *   *   *   *   *   *

10

MALCOLM PULLED UP SHORT ON PAGE 10 OF THE *Golden Valley Gardening Guide* on this day in 1983. The fellow pointing at a warted hubbard squash was his high-school principal. "You can be anything you want," he had written in Malcolm's yearbook a week before graduation. Malcolm wished he had been more specific. Adhesive tape was still holding the two broken parts of Mr. Duncan's glasses together at the bridge. He preferred the acorn for taste, but the warted hubbard was the king of squashes. Malcolm couldn't see Mr. Duncan's feet in the picture, but he bet he was wearing argyles and brown penny-loafers.

On page 17 of the *Golden Valley Gardening Guide* was Jane Fonda beaming in all her suntanned splendor at the Orange Blimp carrot. It was drought-resistant and prolific. "Plenty for the rabbits," she said. Across the page was Waylon Jennings leaning on a hoe thinking that the Jerusalem artichoke was the vegetable of the future. On page 18 was Earl Butz, mellowed out, not a racist bone in his body now, and he believed in beets, the only thing he had in common with the Russians, he said.

*   *   *   *   *   *   *   *   *   *

11

ON THIS DAY IN 1983 *MARGARET'S TREES AND Fruits* appeared in Malcolm Finders' mailbox. Uncle Ted was on page 12. The last he had heard, Ted was down in New Mexico trying to get rich. He was always trying to get rich. He stayed right at the edge of criminality, Malcolm's mother said. Here he was claiming that six of Margaret's Mirrored Ruby strawberries made a pint but they were ever so sweet. Had the black sheep of Malcolm's mother's side of the family turned over a new leaf? Four pages on, Malcolm saw his father. Look at him, just look at him: dead these many years, but there he was, leaning slightly toward the side window of his grain truck piled high with a load of Gold Rush hybrid sweet corn. His ship had finally come in.

*   *   *   *   *   *   *   *   *   *

12

TODAY IN 1983 MALCOLM FINDERS DIDN'T MAKE IT past page 10 of *Great Heartland Select Seeds*. There was the most familiar face he knew. It was himself. He had never looked healthier. It was late summer and Malcolm was standing in the middle of his garden, which stretched away to the horizon. His eyes were on the distance, beyond the camera. He was glowing with absolute happiness.

How did he get there? And why did he ever leave?

*   *   *   *   *   *   *   *   *   *

13

This day brought to you by ROUGHHOUSE COSMETICS, the daring makeup for men who shuffle papers and sign their name all day. If you're being taken for a pushover because you polish your shoes and wear nice suits and carry a briefcase, you're ready for ROUGHHOUSE COSMETICS: they'll make you look as tough as you feel.

A Roughhouse consultant can show you how to brush Brawny Bruise along your jawline, how to pencil in scars and blemishes, how to apply cuts and warts—and they'll all look as natural as if you'd got them in a hockey game or a fight in a bar.

ROUGHHOUSE COSMETICS—when feeling tough is not enough.

*   *   *   *   *   *   *   *   *   *

14

ON VALENTINE'S DAY HAROLD AND ETHEL MIRE
always celebrate the anniversary of their first date, which occurred
on this day in 1958, when they were teenagers. It just happened
to be Valentine's Day. They had driven to town in the '49 Ford
Harold's grandma had loaned to him. They saw a Kirk Douglas
movie called *The Vikings*. In 1973 Harold had located that same
'49 Ford in the machine shed of his grandma's old place and had
hauled it home. The engine was seized and the body was shot. But
Harold had fixed up the interior so that once a year he and Ethel
could brush away the spiderwebs and climb into the front seat to
pretend they were in the cemetery where they parked that first
night so long ago to talk about their future.

Out there in the dusty dark of the old coupe in 1988, the
thirtieth anniversary of that date, they had kissed and hugged a
little, as usual, and had talked about the rest of their future, which
they hoped would be about the same. And then they went back in
the house.

*   *   *   *   *   *   *   *   *   *

15

ON THIS DAY NOT THAT LONG AGO HAROLD MIRE
was in the Coast to Coast store and ran into Howie Humde, the
owner and operator of Walleye Phone Company, which, in a manner of speaking, serves Harold's area. Once Howie gets anybody
cornered, he tends to tell you more than you want to know about
almost anything, but especially the phone business, which has been
up and down for him ever since he started his company on a
shoestring in the summer of '84. "How's it going then?" was all
Harold said. It was all he had to say.

This is what Howie said as Harold kept shifting his weight from
one leg to the other:

"Not too bad. Been out of town, though. Went to New York.
Telecommunications meeting for small-time outfits like mine. The
subject was trunk-line management. It was real interesting. See,

trunk lines are the lines between switching stations. The way it works is, if you call Duluth from St. Paul, your number goes through a local switching station and then is transferred to the trunk line and then it ends up in the Duluth switcher that sends it to the party you called. That's as simple as I can make it. We spent four days on it out there. I took a lot of notes. Eventually Walleye Phone's gonna have some trunk lines to manage, so it was useful information.

"Mack went with me. He's my service specialist, as you know. Tootie stayed behind to hold down the fort. We thought about flying out, but we booked too late to get the cheap fares, so we took Mack's pickup.

"It was a pretty smooth trip. We did have to throw on a rebuilt starter in Erie, Pennsylvania. We took the northern route because we wanted to hit Niagara Falls. It was worth it.

"On the way back we blew a radiator hose coming around Chicago during rush hour. We taped the hose up and put in a gallon of orange drink and two liters of Coke, which was all the liquid we had with us. Nobody stopped to help, not that we needed any. It could have been our imagination, but we thought the cars were actually speeding up and seeing how close they could get to us. Mack said he'd felt safer when he went through army training with live ammo in Texas and was jumping out of cargo planes.

"We did a little sightseeing in New York. Went to the top of the Empire State Building. It made my knees weak to look out. If I were in charge of the world, my tall buildings would go down into the ground, not above it.

"I suppose somebody's already told you about the bad luck we had with the Walleye Phone van. Mack was alone on a service call, which is nothing new. Somebody's sheep got loose and knocked down a pole and ate about a hundred yards of insulation off of a line over by Tinken. Mack pulled off on the shoulder to take care of some personal business—he drinks too much coffee I think— and left the motor running, but he didn't set the parking brake. He figured it must've been going close to fifty miles an hour when it went up over the railing of the bridge and flipped into the Minnesota River. About two weeks later a hunter found the van on the bank by the Bingo Curve when the water went down. Two real nice northerns were stranded in the cab with a couple of huge carp.

"But enough of the negative, Harold. I've gotta get out of here, because we're right at the beginning of a new incentive program

we call Walleye Perks. If you sign up with Walleye you get valuable
gifts. For instance, if we install single-party service or you buy a
second phone from us you get a fifty-pound bag of pork stretcher.
Or you can choose the fifty-pound bag of birdseed instead, and we
throw in a bird feeder."

And with that, Howie left abruptly. Harold had forgotten what
he came into the Coast to Coast for in the first place, so he went
home empty-handed.

*   *   *   *   *   *   *   *   *   *

16

MINNESOTA BIGFOOT WAS SIGHTED SITTING ON THE
front row at a benefit reading for the *Tormented Muse Quarterly*
on this evening in 1986. The first four poets sounded the same to
him, sort of dry and monotonous. But he perked right up when the
dramatic storyteller took the stage and collected himself briefly and
launched into frantic and touching descriptions of the first several
times he had fallen in love. His arms were waving, he was high-
stepping, his voice was up and down. Bigfoot couldn't have slept
if he'd tried. The best part came in the petting sequence—the arms
of the dramatist were flailing. He was ecstatic. His right hand came
around during the breast portion of his presentation and caught
him on his own nose, which started bleeding. And then his left
hand came around involuntarily and he sucker-punched himself
and down he went. Bigfoot was on his two big feet applauding as
the *Tormented Muse* personnel rushed by to resuscitate the per-
former. Bigfoot didn't think the remaining artists on the program
could top that, so he left.

*   *   *   *   *   *   *   *   *   *

17

ON THIS DAY IN 1988 THE MINNEAPOLIS MALL AND
Sports Consortium issued three Whereases:

1. Whereas we have torn down the Met Stadium in Bloomington and built the Humphrey Dome, we now propose erecting
an outdoor stadium for the Twins in Minneapolis on the present

site of the Convention Center which is under construction on the site where we tore down the Minneapolis auditorium. This should create 3,000 new jobs and bring in $500 million annually.

2. Whereas the Humphrey Dome has lived out its useful life, we propose deflating it and hauling it to Bloomington for souvenir seekers and building in its place Triple Trade Towers. This should create 8,000 new jobs and bring in $100 million annually, not to mention thousands of foreign dignitaries on trade missions.

3. Whereas St. Paul is dull, although we give them credit for trying to better themselves, we propose annexing St. Paul and then demolishing the downtown area and building on the site the largest domed mall in the world, with indoor skiing, skydiving, surfing, and camping on artificial grass next to the largest indoor lake in the world. The mall would contain the largest indoor family farm, complete with a working farm family, and the largest indoor mortgage and the lowest indoor prices for the crops. It would contain 15 motels, 6,700 shops and boutiques, 137 restaurants, 800 movie theatres. We conservatively estimate that the St. Paul Domed Mall would create 2,000,000 new jobs and bring in untold billions annually.

* * * * * * * * * *

18 HAROLD MIRE HEARD ON THE RADIO TODAY IN 1987 that three pounds of garbage was generated by every man, woman, and child in the United States every day. There was a man, a woman, and a child in the Mire family, so Harold started weighing their garbage. On the first day they had two empty soup cans weighing four ounces. The orange rinds and outer leaves of the lettuce went on the compost heap and would eventually go on the garden. This was not garbage. The labels had been taken off the cans and burned with the other burnable trash, which totaled fourteen ounces because there were two cardboard boxes in it. The next day they had no throwaways except for the paper sack the apples came in.

After a week of carefully weighed garbage generation, the Mire family was behind the national average by sixty-one pounds. And that included the olive bottle and the peanut-butter jar that Harold had weighed to be fair, even though he washed them and crushed them for use in concrete when he had enough broken glass for a big project.

By the end of the year the Mires would be behind by 3,172 pounds. At that rate, it meant that in the seventeen years they had been living on the building site they had got behind by 53,924 pounds. Twenty-seven tons!!! They'd never catch up with the national average, Harold said, unless they started a public landfill.

*   *   *   *   *   *   *   *   *   *

19

A RETIRED COUPLE FROM EDEN PRAIRIE WAS captured at their snowbird location in Arizona and installed in the Primate Wing of the Minnesota Zoo on this day in 1988. In the natural habitat of a trailer home on the edge of a desert—which contained real scorpions, black widows, fire ants, and poisonous toads—the couple outdrew all previous exhibits, including the Beluga whales and the stockbrokers. In late March they were released back into the wild of their three-bedroom rambler in Eden Prairie.

*   *   *   *   *   *   *   *   *   *

20

TODAY IN 1955 HAROLD MIRE BROUGHT HOME HIS first shop project from high school. It had been conceived in joy as a lamp about three feet tall, involving some one-by-sixes formed into an X as seen from the top. In its completed form, the frayed electrical cord ran up one of the crevices and entered the socket assembly, which was loose even before the kids on the school bus pounced on it.

Due to some last-minute sawing of the base in the shop room to get a C− from the teacher and to keep it from looking like the leaning lamp of Pisa, the project was only eighteen inches high when he carried it into the living room. Harold knew the lamp was awful, yet he was unable to keep from propping it up on the table next to the couch.

When his father saw it he was speechless, and also, it would be fair to say, aghast. Harold's mother immediately sized up the sit-

uation and said, "Oh, that's nice." Everybody noticed she didn't
say nice *what*.

The lamp never once made the darkness light, because nobody
would plug it in, and after five weeks it disappeared forever. Harold
never became much handier with wood and has always steered
away from devices that are meant to illuminate.

*   *   *   *   *   *   *   *   *   *

21

THE COMIC VAGRANCY LAW WENT INTO EFFECT IN
the Twin Cities today in 1986, making stand-up comedy routines
in public places a felony. Performing in comedy clubs was not
punishable by law, however. The vagrancy law was the result of
an epidemic practice by local comedians of working bank lobbies,
checkout lines at K Mart, foyers of churches. They were even
standing up in city buses and doing their routines. You couldn't
turn around without somebody starting a show on you:

"Hey. Look, am I funny or what? Didja see the newspaper
today? Are you kidding me? Huh, huh?"

Most people feel that the comic vagrancy law led directly to
the Great Twin Cities Comedy War of 1988.

*   *   *   *   *   *   *   *   *   *

22

HAROLD MIRE WAS HOME ALONE AT NOON ON THIS
day in 1986 and decided to have tomato soup. The Campbell's
label still said to add one can of water or milk, but when Harold
was growing up his mother made it with two cans of milk, or even
three cans if he had friends over. From the first day it was served
to him, Harold had loved milky tomato soup with saltines crushed
into it to form a pale-pink, gummy mass that would hold a spoon
straight up in it.

Harold's mother had often served the tomato soup with a toasted
cheese sandwich made with Kleenex bread, which was white bread
that, if you squeezed a slice of it in your fist, became a moist ball
indistinguishable from a wadded-up used Kleenex. As an adult,
Harold knew all about natural low-salt whole-wheat bread and

that's what he mostly ate, even though it made him whinny sometimes and paw his front feet in the dirt. But he kept a stash of
Kleenex bread in a brown bag in the bottom of the freezer in case
he got the urge to slap some Velveeta between two slices and put
it under the oven broiler until it looked like a charcoal briquet. He
knew his mother's recipe by heart. It was a great sandwich.

While the soup was heating, Harold went to the freezer. He
also had a frozen slab of Velveeta hidden in there. Who said you
can't go home again?

*   *   *   *   *   *   *   *   *   *   *

23

ON THIS DAY IN 1987 MINNESOTA BIGFOOT WAS
sighted at a supermarket in St. Louis Park, where he was the proud
winner of a two-minute shopping spree at Crazy Days. The manager told him to remember the contest rules: only six meat items
could be selected. At the buzzer, Bigfoot loped into the cooler at
the back of the store and brought out six sides of beef and piled
them on the cart and still had thirty seconds left to put two dozen
family-size boxes of frozen Tater Tots, a head of lettuce, and a
bottle of Creamy Italian dressing on the rack under the cart. Bigfoot
had bent the rules, but the manager reached up and put his arm
on Bigfoot's shoulder for the photo session anyway.

*   *   *   *   *   *   *   *   *   *

24

CABIN FEVER TAKES MANY FORMS BUT ON THIS
Saturday in 1986, Harold Mire almost got out his collection of
National Geographic maps so he could study in detail some of the
places he wanted to visit but probably never would in this lifetime.
But that even sounded gloomy to him, so he took the positive
approach and decided to make his own maps: he would chart the
territory he knew best. Maybe he would find mystery in it again.

Using colored pencils and a long sheet of newsprint off the stub
roll in the garage, Harold began with the desert region of the living
room, with its nostril-searing heat rising from the Floor Furnace,
and the static sparks that could strike without warning if you shuf-

fled too much on the Matted Green Carpet. The main highway
(heavy red) came in from the kitchen and branched off (thin red)
to the two bedrooms. The blacktopped county roads (black) led to
the Erratic Record Player, the Sloping Couch, and other points of
interest. The township roads (black and white, segmented for
gravel) led to minor attractions, such as the "Spot Where He Spilled
the Spaghetti Sauce in 1973," or the "Four Deep Depressions" in
the carpet.

"A heavily populated area by day [Harold wrote], bustling with
traffic, the Living Room at night is full of shadows and silence. A
tiny mouse lives behind the piano, but that's about it for animal
life, except for the spiders behind the bookshelf and the millions
of microbes that dwell in the carpet and never leave home."

Harold drew in the main highway through the kitchen and
followed it to the Northern Plateau region of the bathroom, with
its Whistling Drafts, its Icy Floors, its Cold Toilet Seat. Harold
crawled on his hands and knees into the farthest reaches of the
Bathroom Closet, a no-man's-land of Boxes, Light Bulbs, and
Clothes in Grocery Sacks.

He took notes with a flashlight because electricity had not come
to the Bathroom Closet. He sketched in the Hanging Garden of
Sports Jackets that he had bought at garage sales or were sold to
him by well-meaning men's clothiers over the years. He had the
best of intentions when it came to suiting up, but his formal ward-
robe always ended up right where he hung it, on permanent exhibit
in the Hanging Garden.

Ethel asked Harold a question from the Bedroom and she heard
a muffled reply and found Harold in the Bathroom Closet, sitting
cross-legged on the floor under the garments, looking at the bleach
bottles and the shoe polish on the shelves, talking to himself and
taking notes. She asked him what he was doing.

Harold said, "I'm mapping the dark regions of the closet for
the first time." He came out and showed her the intricate map of
the living room.

That was really it for her—she was afraid he might just go all
the way around the bend this time. Ethel forced Harold to call up
his friends and have a poker game.

Not one of the guys had trouble getting permission to leave the
house. They were dealing by noon and they played until dawn at
the Great Round Oak Kitchen Table. Many trips were made to

the Loud Refrigerator with the Clunk, and to the Northern Plateau.

*   *   *   *   *   *   *   *   *   *

25

HAROLD MIRE WAS SITTING IN A LAWN CHAIR AND wearing his parka at the edge of his property on this day in 1986 when he caught a whiff of something on the wind that smelled exactly like the Bumby Bakery, where he worked when he was nineteen years old, in 1958. His assignment was buns and rolls. Harold spent most of his shift on the bun extruder and couldn't help but watch the guy on the bread-wrapping machine across from him, Ernie something, who was a one-man show.

Whenever Ernie sneezed, which was about every thirty minutes, he turned it into a major production, with bent-over prancing foreplay and then a three-second blast that he always vocalized into the same stretched word. They could easily hear it through the walls at the mortuary next door. HOOORRRRRSSSSSSSE-SSSHHHHHIIIIIT!!!!! Between sneezes he would usually get in one session of Academy Award–quality butt scratching. Harold's opinion was that Ernie's talents were wasted at the bakery—he should have gone into pro football.

*   *   *   *   *   *.   *   *   *   *

26

ON ANY GIVEN FEBRUARY DAY IN MINNESOTA—AND this one in 1988 was no different—nearly two hundred married couples decide to finish their basement in the spring, or at least make it livable, but after they go down there and screw the bulbs in to get some light because the switches are shot, and push a few moldy paper boxes around so they can measure for the indoor/outdoor carpet (purple would be nice), and they bonk their foreheads into three or four hefty spiders hanging from the joists, and step in the sludge from the water heater, and are frightened by their Boeing 737 furnace when it fires up for takeoff, they decide to unscrew the bulbs and go back upstairs and shut the door. Maybe a screened porch is what they want.

*   *   *   *   *   *   *   *   *   *

27

MIDMORNING ON THIS DAY IN 1988 HAROLD MIRE was 2.5 miles from home, jogging on a gravel township road, when he passed a wet spot in the compacted dirt. He knew it was not the result of melting snow, because the temperature had fallen to near zero in the night and the sun was not yet hot enough at 10:30 to create a soaking of the ground. Besides the road was clear of ice and snow.

Harold decided to go on across the highway and out to the 4.5-mile mark (the Rugges' mailbox). It would mean jogging nine miles, but it would give him time to consider the implications of the wet spot, a rough circle about a foot in diameter. A half-mile before the wet spot, Harold now remembered, he had seen the dust of a vehicle coming his way from behind the small hill where he would find the wet spot. But no vehicle had materialized.

This is what Harold speculated: On his second pass by the wet spot, if he found tire tracks indicating that a vehicle had stopped and turned around, the mystery was solved. The gravel road's intersection with the highway was only a third of a mile beyond the wet spot. Obviously, somebody's teeth had been floating.

Harold slowed up and circled the evidence, almost jogging in place. The driver might as well have left a note. The vehicle had pulled up, the driver had got out and taken care of business and had then executed a U-turn and headed back to the highway for points unknown.

Harold knew that if he conducted a further examination of the site, very little else would be revealed about the car and the man driving it. *Or the woman*: There was not enough evidence to determine gender. Not even the position of the footprints was conclusive. That's what Harold liked about jogging alone in the country, the little mysteries that illuminated his day.

*   *   *   *   *   *   *   *   *   *

28

AT A SECOND-FLOOR AEROBIC-DANCE STUDIO ON
this day in 1987, Minnesota Bigfoot was sighted in leotards and
Reeboks. He didn't stick out all that much, because he was also
wearing a muscle shirt, purple leg-warmers around his ankles,
sweatbands on his wrists, and a headband that said "Go for It."
After having everybody work on their tushes for a while, DeeDee
put on a Heavy Metal tape to pick up the pace. Bigfoot crashed
through a weak spot in the floor during an improvised leap and
dropped into a vat of taco salad in the deli on the first floor and
was later sighted being pursued by a police officer on a decoy
operation.

*   *   *   *   *   *   *   *   *   *

29

ON THIS LEAP YEAR DAY IN 1988 HAROLD MIRE
decided it was time to straighten the storm door on the guest shed.
Actually it had been time since the summer of 1987 when the wind
had caught it and sprung it. What should I fix today? he had, as
usual, asked himself at breakfast. *Storm door* was the answer that
came to him.

Harold put on his old ragged Air Force parka that Ethel had
tried to throw out last year and grabbed a few tools and stood
in the bitter wind and removed the doorjamb and shimmed it
and stood back and admired how tight the door was now. This was
when he noticed the warmth on his right thigh and looked down
to see smoke coming out of the pants pocket he had shoved
the pliers into. How could this be? He slapped his pocket to stop
the fire and then pulled out the charred contents. Besides the
undamaged pliers, he found two matchbooks. The matches in one
book had all ignited at once; the other matchbook was closed. It
was baffling, but not for long. Harold's policy of carrying only
safety matches in his pocket was wise, but one of his other policies, making sure to have a spare of everything so you didn't
run out, was not so wise. One book of matches had opened itself

and a match from it had rubbed on the striker of the closed book. Harold developed a new policy on matches and Ethel sewed a two-inch patch over the charred hole in the pocket of his work pants. It could have been worse. In 1992 he would be more careful on this day.

* * * * * * * * * * *

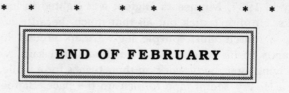

END OF FEBRUARY

MARCH

1 MAYBE START AN AQUARIUM TODAY BECAUSE exhaustive studies have shown that the presence of fish in a house lowers the blood pressure and reduces stress, unless you live near a river that floods every year and the dike around your place doesn't hold up and you have a basement full of Minnesota game fish which the Department of Natural Resources won't let you keep because it is considered trapping even if flooding is an act of God. You can't win for losing.

* * * * * * * * * *

2 IF YOU DID BUY AN AQUARIUM YESTERDAY AND SET it up, I'm sure you're happy with how neat and clean it looks and how the fish are so peaceful in their miniature environment, and why didn't you think of this before. It's changing the whole way you look at life. You are considering having an aquarium in every room in the house. You think of becoming a volunteer spokesperson for the home-aquarium industry and helping people turn themselves around. You think about starting a fish club at the community center. Maybe you'll give out pamphlets at work and talk to your colleagues around the Coke machine.

* * * * * * * * * *

3 ANOTHER DAY WITH THE AQUARIUM DAWNS AND while Mr. Coffee is chugging away out there by the toaster, you are totally relaxed by the rhythmic motion of the tropical fish, but you notice flecks of green on the inside of the aquarium glass. Algae. You get the whole family in to look at it. It's a wonderful thing, you tell them: this closed system has begun to grow. "It's like the beginning of time. What we are witnessing here is a universal pattern that illustrates the essential rationality and goodness of nature. There's hope for us all, peace is possible." The family applauds.

* * * * * * * * * *

4 AQUARIUM WATCH, DAY FOUR: THE FILTER SYSTEM malfunctions but you catch it after only a gallon of water siphons onto the carpet. The problem was some kind of greenish-reddish slime plugging the tubes of the filter. The pump sounds funny. One of the tiger fish is belly up over in the corner by the heater. After a brief discussion with the family about whether fish have souls, you drop the little fellow in the garbage. You are haunted all day by this.

* * * * * * * * * *

5 MORE BEAUTIFUL PRIMORDIAL ALGAE HAVE FORMED on the inside of the glass on Day Five of the Aquarium Watch. You can only see the fish by raising the lid and looking in from the top. The gravel at the bottom of the tank is covered with a layer of churning dark stuff. The artificial plants are all pinkish-green and have feathery growths. You keep going outside to see why the plane is flying so low over the house, but it's the aquarium air pump, which is vibrating and periodically hopping around the room at the end of its power cord.

* * * * * * * * * *

6 IN THE NIGHT YOU HAVE CREPT INTO THE LIVING room and unplugged the air pump, because you have an important planning meeting and can't afford to lose the sleep, but you don't sleep anyway because of the gurgling, which stops just about the time your alarm goes off. When you get up you see that the water has turned into a green Jell-O–like substance and the angelfish and mollies are all suspended in it and not moving. They look worse than you feel. You plug the pump back in before the rest of the family wanders in, but it makes only one WHOOMPY sound and expires.

* * * * * * * * * *

7

HAVING CARRIED THE AQUARIUM OUT BEHIND THE garage, you deliver a brief message to the family today about the laws of nature, and inevitability, and how at least they were with us for seven days, and then you commit the aquarium and its gelatinized miniature environment to the earth, but the younger kids are off riding their bikes by this time and don't hear your stirring conclusion and the older kids are rolling their eyes.

*　*　*　*　*　*　*　*　*　*

8

This day and the one following it are sponsored by **BIGGER HAMMER HARDWARE,** formed in a Quonset hut in Roseville, Minnesota, in 1984 to fill the void for the handyman who gets in over his head but is afraid to call just anybody. The naked truth is that if you do it yourself, sooner or later you're going to need a board stretcher or a bigger hammer. And sometimes you saw it twice and it's still too short. Known throughout the Gopher State as the handyperson's pals, BIGGER HAMMER field representatives make housecalls in unmarked cars and wear unmarked clothing. And best of all they're just as friendly as your next-door neighbor but without all that sarcasm that hurts so much when you're trying to do your very best. By this day in 1988, BIGGER HAMMER had outlets in thirty Minnesota cities.

*　*　*　*　*　*　*　*　*　*

9

THE FIRST HOME HANDYMAN GIVES BIGGER HAMMER Hardware a call on this day after seeing their ad in the Roseville *Shopper.* The following is a personal testimony from a valiant do-it-yourselfer whose name has been changed to Bert to protect him from ridicule for his innocent and well-meaning home-repair fiasco. It's no crime to foul up when you do it yourself.

☞BERT'S STORY

I remember the time the old water heater in the basement got to leaking around the bottom. Steam coming up through the floor in the bedroom was the first sign of trouble. I guess I should have set up a regular schedule of water-heater inspections. But a guy tends to let things go—you know how that is. When I went downstairs, I had to wear my trout waders, not that it did that much good, because I got tangled up in a bicycle I couldn't see through the murky water and soaked myself real good when I took the plunge. A dead mouse was floating around over by the canned tomatoes and there was a musty odor that made me lightheaded.

But my dizziness and depression didn't last long. Once I had unplugged the drain with the Twisto-Snake and got my hands on the right tools, installing a new water heater seemed like a piece of cake. You see, basically what you got is your inlet side, where the cold water comes in, and your outlet side, where the hot water comes out. It's simple, but when you're down there in the cellar in the glow of a trouble light, you can drift into a dream state. That's what I like about being a home handyman. That sense of peace and understanding that comes from interacting with a physical system.

The first thing that came up, I had to bash in the top of the new water heater with the sledgehammer so it would fit through the door of the cellar. It looked a little rough, but it didn't hurt the working parts and only reduced the capacity by three or four gallons. But the deal was, after I installed it and turned the main valve back on, we had lukewarm water coming out of all the faucets except the shower, which was ice cold. And when I flushed the toilet an eight-foot Yellowstone Park–style hot geyser erupted from the bowl area. I was glad I had sent the family off to the mall for the day. So I took my soggy hat in hand and called the Bigger Hammer people and a guy came right out. He told me not to feel bad: he'd seen one other water-heater installation that was worse than mine. I really appreciated that.

*　　*　　*　　　*　　　*　　*　　　*　　　*　　*　　*

10

ON THIS DAY IN 1988 THE LEGISLATURE DESIGNATED the Niceguy as the official Minnesota State burglar trap. It is a simple and nonviolent burglar deterrent and works without all the noise and carpet stains associated with the conventional heavy jaw-type burglar traps. The homeowner sets the bait—a couple of rare coins or a diamond ring—in the telephone-booth-size acrylic enclosure, and when the burglar walks in to take the bait, the door closes gently behind him. In the morning the homeowner can either call the local SPCB or release the burglar back into the neighborhood with a little lecture and a handshake.

*   *   *   *   *   *   *   *   *   *

11

THE MINNESOTA STATE LEGISLATURE TRIED TO PASS a resolution on this day in 1987 to make the deck the official state home appendage, after a survey showed that more Gopher State homeowners add a deck to the side of their houses than don't, whether they need one or not. In order to qualify as a state deck, the Legislature decided that a deck must:

1. Be at least two and a half feet off the ground outside your house but can be as high as thirty feet up if you have it jutting from your remodeled attic room.
2. Be on stilts so that dogs, skunks, escaped criminals, and children can crawl under there, and so bikes and wagons can disappear.
3. Be at least ten by ten feet square, but it may be three times the square footage of your house if so desired.

*   *   *   *   *   *   *   *   *

12

THE DECK RESOLUTION CAME WITHIN A HAIR OF passing in the Legislature on this day in 1987 after vigorous debate established four more qualifying rules. To be designated an official state deck, with seal and governor's signature, the deck must also:

4. Slope slightly but never at more than a thirty-degree angle.

5. Be able to withstand a gale-force wind so it doesn't end up on top of your neighbor's deck.

6. Be used at least three times a week in summer even if you only read the paper out there, or drink your coffee, or pose casually in deck clothing for your neighbors and pretend to be enjoying yourself.

And furthermore:

7. If at any time you enclose the deck and put in windows so you can be out there when it is too wet, too dry, too hot, too cold, too noisy, or too dusty, your deck will lose its deck status and become a porch, which is a thing of the past.

*   *   *   *   *   *   *   *   *

13

AFTER HOUSE REPUBLICAN DIVET DOLE FOUGHT TO have Rule No. 8 added to the deck legislation on this day in 1987, the resolution passed with cheering and handshakes all around. Another day, another dollar.

8. In winter you must bundle up and stand out there and look off in the distance once a week, although if it's windy you are allowed to lash yourself to the deck with a rope so you don't skate across the icy surface and flip over the flimsy waist-high rail.

*   *   *   *   *   *   *   *   *

14

BECAUSE THEY FIGURED THEY WERE ON A ROLL, THE State Legislature on this day in 1987 reprimanded Minnesota homeowners because the housing survey that led to the landmark deck resolution also revealed that people were using their recreation rooms in the basement less and less and storing paper boxes full of junk down there again more and more, and in far too many cases standing at the top of the stairs and throwing stuff down without even turning on the light.

*   *   *   *   *   *   *   *   *   *

15 ON THIS DAY IN 1988 MINNESOTA BIGFOOT GOT HIS fill of media exposure. He was sighted on a panel of hairy experts on "Twin Cities Live" in the morning, and then in the afternoon hosts Steve and Sharon used him for a grooming experiment on "Good Company." The audience thought he didn't look any better after the lady from Hair Ball, Inc., was through with him. In the evening Bigfoot was sighted glancing over his shoulder on a Minneapolis street: the Channel 4 I-Team was just beginning what they hoped would be a weeklong exposé of this fraud. But Bigfoot lost them.

*   *   *   *   *   *   *   *   *   *

16 ON THIS DAY IN 1984 HAROLD MIRE SAW HIS FRIEND Stephen at the hardware store. Harold was looking for expansion bolts to hold the sliding shower-door frame of his new shower stall in so it wouldn't fall out every time he knocked his head on the top rail. It had come with some permanent sticky tape to hold it in, but that only lasted two weeks, which was about par for permanent these days. Stephen asked Harold's opinion on several items he meant to install in the new house he and Lois were planning to build. This is a synopsis of the conversation:

☞**STEPHEN**   ☞**HAROLD**

Garbage disposal: A crime against civilization. There's no way you should grind up perfectly good garbage and send it to a sewage plant when you could have a compost heap.

Dishwasher: Are you kidding me? It's a crime against
                         civilization. Do you think we'd be where
                         we are today if our foremothers had had
                         dishwashers? Those things are an abom-
                         ination. If you ever see me with a dish-
                         washer in any house of mine, you can
                         sign me up for the bowling team—it'll
                         be all over.

Jacuzzi: Same as a hot tub in my book. You
                         should never have anything in your
                         house that would be the last thing you
                         would ever have if you had any sense.
                         You've got to stop someplace on this
                         long march toward the ridiculous in so-
                         called modern living, and I stop a long
                         way before Jacuzzis. I don't even be-
                         lieve in carpet, but I suppose you got
                         yourself scheduled for a whole houseful.
                         I can see deep shag in your eyes.

Stephen thanked Harold for his wonderful advice and said he
would see him at the poker game Friday night, if not before.

Harold was known for his opinions; his friends were known for
paying very little attention to them.

*   *   *   *   *   *   *   *   *

17

CHET KEVINSON FARMS NEAR A TOWN THAT COULD
be mentioned, but won't be. On this day in 1978, Chet was the
first farmer to plant corn in Minnesota. It was true that the overnight temperatures had been below freezing for almost a week, but
Chet had a sixth sense when it came to corn planting, and what he
sensed was a real warming trend that would give him the leap on
his neighbors.

At 4:00 in the afternoon, a mile from home in the north 180,
planting like a madman, Chet was caught by a blinding blizzard
he would have had a warning about if he had fixed his tractor radio

during his winter idle time, but he hadn't. By 11:00 that night, it had let up enough so a guy could see beyond the tractor cab. It took Chet five minutes to get out of the tractor and more than an hour to leap and tumble and fall home through the field in the deep snow. He almost froze his sixth sense off.

*   *   *   *   *   *   *   *   *   *

18

CHET KEVINSON MADE THE NATIONAL NEWSPAPERS on this day in 1978 in an Associated Press photo that showed the air cleaner and exhaust stack of his tractor sticking up in a field of white. You can't see the planter. "Chet Kevinson gets an early corn-planting start in Minnesota," it said under the picture. The same photo was placed on page 30 of his town's Centennial Book in 1985. Chet knew he would never live it down. He was still farming the same place in 1988. He just lets it run off his back. He can take it, even in mid-February, when the sit-down comedians drinking coffee at the elevator office start in on him: *I don't know why you're hanging around here, Chet, when you could be out there clearing your fields with a snowblower.* Pretty funny.

*   *   *   *   *   *   *   *   *   *

19

THE ICE WENT OUT OF THE BOXELDER CITY LAKE this day in 1988. Boxelder residents said it seemed like that fifty-mile-an-hour west wind sort of got a hold on the pocked surface and the next thing you knew there was nothing but open water and the beach on the east was a jumble of cheesy ice. The water turned an unearthly green, the color of the crystals that used to be in Jar No. 7 of the Master Chemistry set every kid wanted for Christmas in the days before large liability suits.

If you mixed Jar No. 9 with No. 10 in those days (which every kid did) you came close to the smell that blew over the two-thirds of Boxelder downwind from the lake. Some citizens called for an emergency evacuation. The experts at the cafe thought maybe a truckload of Sani-Flush and a big brush would take care of it.

*   *   *   *   *   *   *   *   *   *

20

"REGARDING THE HORRIBLE STINK RISING FROM the lake," began the letter from Mayor Roger Doan to the citizens of Boxelder this day in 1988.

Let me explain it this way to those of you who seem to think I'm responsible. Say you have a hot tub with whirlpool—which I don't, so use your own. What you do is throw ten or fifteen dead carp and bullheads into the bottom of the hot tub and then let the whole thing freeze for about three months, and then you heat it up again and start the whirlpool. What you'd have is a rotten, foam-covered liquid no different than the stuff some of you will be water-skiing on in about six weeks and swear you're having a good time. I wouldn't even put my feet in it wearing galoshes. And anybody swimming in it should do estate planning first.

Well, pardon us, people said. Sure it stunk to high heaven, but it wasn't the end of the world. It was obvious that Roger had suffered burnout as mayor and wasn't up to dealing with the crisis. There would have to be a special election now to pick somebody else to bless with the $50 a month and the $10 for every council meeting. Maybe they could bump it to $60 if the new mayor would also set up a fact-finding lake committee.

* * * * * * * * * * *

21

GALEN JOHNSON, ROUTE 2, BOXELDER, MINNESOTA, received a chain letter today in 1987 that said if he broke the chain or even made fun of it the sweated joints in his copper plumbing system would begin leaking one by one, starting with the supposedly solid connections in the upstairs bathroom. That made him feel better, because he didn't have an upstairs bathroom or an upstairs. The letter went on to say that if Galen shipped a used but useful object to the Minnesota person at the bottom of the list and added his name to the top of the list and sent the letter off to six other people he would reap untold riches in similar stuff.

Galen immediately mailed Abel Torgery a used power-steering pump from the '69 AMC Rebel he had permanently parked in the second row of his vehicle collection back in '85, when it threw a rod at 183,421 heroic miles. The right guy would be tickled to get it. But Galen didn't stand down by the mailbox and hold his breath.

* * * * * * * * *

22 **This day is brought to you and paid for by SERVANT CARD,** the credit card with the difference. When you walk into a store and ask, "Do you take SERVANT CARD here?," if you're lucky they'll say, "Nope, never heard of it." That means you can walk right out of there empty-handed and home free. SERVANT CARD is not good for credit purchases in thousands of stores across the nation. It can save you a bundle. Keep your cash in the bank and carry SERVANT CARD. It's hardly accepted anywhere, and all for one low monthly charge. And for special qualified customers, save even more with the exclusive GOLDEN SILVER SERVANT CARD—guaranteed to be absolutely good for nothing anyplace in the world. It's not even worth stealing.

* * * * * * * * *

23 THIS DAY IS THE BEGINNING OF THE MOSQUITO SEASON inside Minnesota restaurants decorated with hanging plants and waterfalls and waiters in Tarzan outfits. It is also the birthday of M. Birdy Morton, inventor of the hydraulic flagpole and nut-cracker.

* * * * * * * * *

24 ON THIS DAY IN 1988 MINNESOTA BIGFOOT WAS sighted at the Zoo with his huge nose pressed against the glass, looking at the new Primate Exhibit: five male poker players with red eyes, beards, and cigars, who dealt hand after hand of seven-card stud. They had been trapped in a basement in St. Cloud and lured into the Zoo van with pastrami sandwiches and cheese curls. The game broke up on April 10 and the boys were allowed to go home and shower.

* * * * * * * * * * *

25

AFTER ONE OF THE MILDEST WINTERS ON RECORD in Minnesota the governor's office released the alarming trade figures on winter humor this day in 1987. Minnesota's overall production of winter humor for local markets had dropped 56 percent, but its exports of winter humor to the other forty-nine states had plummeted 98 percent.

And what was worse, most of the winter humor wasn't all that funny, either: "It's been so snowless and warm this winter, I didn't tie an avalanche cord to my car so I could find it in the parking lot" just did not have the old kick to it. But what really hurt the winter-humor trade balance was the tough winter experienced on the East Coast. It was so bad that for the first time in history New Yorkers pulled ahead of Minnesotans in winter-humor production. It was a sad day for the Gopher State.

But luckily, by this same day in 1988, a long gruesome winter had made Minnesotans happy again and as funny as ever.

* * * * * * * * * *

26

THE BOXELDER ROUTE 2 CARRIER, CORKY COGDAHL, called Galen Johnson at 7:30 this morning in 1987 to see if he'd be home, because Corky had a few packages for him that wouldn't fit in the box and some of them were dripping. Corky also wondered what the deal was, and since Galen had a sneaking suspicion that chain packages were as illegal as chain letters, he told Corky he had ordered a few parts for the old Massey Ferguson.

Galen unwrapped and evaluated these untold used riches:

Fan belt (heavy-duty; from a riding mower, he guessed)
Coiled remnant of electric fence wire
Water pump (probably Chrysler)
Three baby-food jars full of wood screws
Camshaft (not labeled, but for a V-8 of some sort)
Seven hacksaw blades (a few teeth missing here and there)
Rear-end gears from a GMC pickup (interesting)
Two sink traps (just the ticket for the basement sink)
Glove-compartment door (VW bug, pre-1975)

* * * * * * * * * *

TODAY IN 1987 CORKY COGDAHL DELIVERED A FEW more chain riches to Galen's place:

Pole lamp (a couple of sockets dangled)
Peanut-butter jar full of washers (random sizes)
Unknown item (probably internal valve of a hydraulic jack)
Speedometer (with chewed cable)
Bicycle derailleur mechanism (six sprockets)
Fuse box (charred, two pennies still inside)
Two dozen aluminum rods (from TV antennas)

* * * * * * * * * *

28 TODAY IN 1987 WHEN CORKY DROPPED THE PACKAGES off up at the house, he said to Galen, "That old Massey Ferguson tractor of yours must be in bad shape."

Galen said, "You know how it is. Everything goes wrong at once."

Today's complete list of riches:

A mayonnaise jar full of stove bolts (no nuts)
Keyed chuck for quarter-inch drill (worn out)
Six sash weights (antiques)
A fruitcake tin full of ball bearings (great resource)

* * * * * * * * * *

29

ABOUT NOON TODAY IN 1987 GALEN JOHNSON HEARD a truck coming up his lane and went outside to find the Gopher Freight driver unloading a thirty-gallon drum full of faucet handles. It was the thrill of a lifetime for Galen.

* * * * * * * * * *

30

THIS DAY IN 1987 (AND EVERY DAY FOREVER AFTER) no chain riches arrived for Galen. Somebody must have broken the chain, because according to Galen's calculations, he should have received six to the sixth power of good used things. He was quite a bit short of that, but nevertheless it was not too bad a return on his investment of a power-steering pump. There was hope for the world yet.

* * * * * * * * * *

31

ALTHOUGH HE DID NOT BELIEVE FOR A MINUTE IN astrology, Harold Mire checked his horoscope this morning in 1988. It said: "A day of surprises. Water will be important. A faroff land will beckon."

A wild-eyed poet in the Arts Kiosk at the State Fair a couple of years back had said that he could tell Harold was a Pisces the minute he walked up to the counter and slapped his dollar down: he knew his type, he said. Harold undoubtedly stayed near the walls at parties, he shopped in supermarkets during off-peak. He also said that Harold had no center to his being, that he would bend with the slightest wind of change.

Free of charge, Harold told the poet he should get a real job and stop spreading animal waste. The bard of the prairies had got one thing right though: grocery shopping. Pisces or not, who in

their right mind would ever shop in a supermarket on Friday afternoon if they could do it on Tuesday morning at 8:30?

Later on this day, Harold drove into town to buy a few bushels
of cracked corn for the horse and decided to stop off at the Mu-
nicipal. That surprised him—he couldn't remember when he had
last dropped in. He got another surprise when he bellied up to the
bar: his cousin Philip was sitting there (that wasn't the surprise)
and he said, "Let me buy you a drink."

Harold said, "Thanks, whatever you're having."

What Philip was having was shots of bar whiskey. Harold held
his breath and threw it down. He had forgotten how much pain
was involved with straight shots. He washed his throat with a glass
of water and ordered a tap of Grain Belt and sipped on it while
he and Philip watched a documentary about Iceland on the TV set
above the potato-chip rack.

It almost made Harold a believer.

*   *   *   *   *   *   *   *   *   *

END OF MARCH

APRIL

1 **This day brought to you by the MEAT LOAF INSTITUTE**
and me, Calvin Lodin, on behalf of the millions of households that
"proudly serve" the dish that was two hundred years old on this
day in 1987. They don't call me Sir Meat Loaf for nothing. I have
devoted my life to this major food group and it disturbs me greatly
to see meat loaf get such bad press. The so-called news media never
fail to print every lurid detail about the few meat-loaf disasters, yet
they never tell the other side of the story. The "60 Minutes" exposé
a couple of weeks ago is a case in point. Meat loaf being tossed
around in backyard football games!!! The Petrified Meat Loaf Forest
in Arizona!!! Cheap shots, and a real disservice to Americans.

Well, the fact is, Mr. Smarty Pants CBS, that meat-loaf failures
are in the minority. How hard can it be to mix ground beef, water,
ketchup, and crushed saltines or bread crumbs or oatmeal together
and press it into a loaf pan and bake it? And even if you put in
too much liquid—a common error with meat loaf if you are asleep
at the switch—and it doesn't set up properly during baking, you
can always save the day and serve it as a *meat shake* in a tall
glass with shaved ice and a large-diameter straw. Thank you. And
the next time you hear somebody bad-mouthing meat loaf, think
about it.

* * * * * * * * * * *

2 THIS IS CLOWN DAY AT THE CAPITOL IN ST. PAUL.
All the elected public servants goof off for eight hours, showing
their constituents that they have a silly, unproductive side.

* * * * * * * * * *

3 BIRTHDAY OF ENTERTAINER AL LARSON, INVENTOR
of the Exer-Tractor, a compact system of pedals, pulleys, cables,
and weights designed to be an integral part of a modern tractor

cab, enabling farmers to listen to their stereo tape decks, do field-work, and get a little exercise at the same time. During the premiere grandstand demonstration of the Exer-Tractor at the Farm Trade Show in Butterdown, Minnesota, in 1979, before a crowd of five hundred farmers, Al got tangled in the neck-conditioner ropes while trying to hook up the lower-leg component and lost control just long enough for the tractor to veer into the side of the Beefo Feed Additive truck.

Al was asked to repeat the performance at 4:00. This was the beginning of a career in show business for Al Larson and the end of the Exer-Tractor, which was voted the worst agricultural invention ever and the most dangerous—a real achievement when one considers the competition in the field.

*   *   *   *   *   *   *   *   *   *

4 HAROLD MIRE WAVED HIS HOMER HANKY ON THIS day in 1988 every time he pulled it out of his back pocket to fluff it up and blow his nose—it was dusty at his place. He knew that this use of the Homer Hanky would appear sacrilegious to other Twins fans who had a safe-deposit box full of World Series memorabilia, but Harold believed in getting his money's worth out of a product. During the All-Star break, Harold planned to wash up his Homer Hanky and iron it and get ready for some germ-free flapping at the Dome. And he did it, because the Twins weren't doing too bad by then.

*   *   *   *   *   *   *   *   *   *

5 THIS IS THE FIRST FAIRLY SAFE DAY IN MINNESOTA to put away your winter clothes and remove the blizzard-survival gear from the trunk of your car: the snow shovel, the sleeping bags, the thermal blankets, the last will and testament, Michener novels, and the rest. Forget about remembering where you stored it all, because next fall you won't, and you'll rummage around for six or seven hours like a madman as usual and still find the stuff in the

last place you look and the mice will have raised three litters in it
in absolute luxury.

*   *   *   *   *   *   *   *   *   *

ON THIS DESIGNATED MAINTENANCE DAY IN 1987
Harold Mire ran the '70 Chrysler Newport into the shade of the
big box-elder tree and slid under it on his back to check out the
leak in the muffler and saw that the two main steel beams of
the frame were almost rusted through. Hit a big bump, it could be
in two pieces. He didn't even want to think about it. The days on
the open road were over for the old prairie schooner. Harold turned
the key one more time and drove the Blue Bomber to the edge of
the grove beyond the garage, with its headlights and grillwork
facing south toward the distant hills of Buffalo Ridge.

From the kitchen window Ethel could see the tail end of the
Chrysler. When Harold wandered in, she said, "You aren't planning
to leave that there are you?"

"What else would I do?"

"Take it to the junkyard."

"It's not junk. Besides I'd be lucky to get twenty-five bucks for
it. It's a member of the family."

*   *   *   *   *   *   *   *   *   *

HAROLD REMOVED THE GAS TANK FROM THE
Chrysler on this day in 1987 and stored it behind the chicken shed
until he was ready to make a crankcase-oil supply tank out of it
for the heater in the ice-fishing house he planned to build out of
some of the scrap lumber he had hauled from Arnie Kevinson's
old barn.

Harold also took off the fuel pump, the carburetor, the alter-
nator, the coil, the regulator, the headlights, the two heads from
the V-8, the fan, the water pump, the radiator, the power-steering
pump, the starter, the distributor, and all the wiring under the
hood. He stored these temporarily on the floor of his shop. He
would organize them later.

*   *   *   *   *   *   *   *   *   *

8

TODAY IN 1987 HAROLD DISMANTLED THE DASH-
board on the Blue Bomber, including all the heater cables, the
ductwork, and the instruments. His main impression was that, even
though we had landed people on the moon, we were still in the
dashboard middle ages. Detroit's principle was to cram it full and
then cover it with plastic and sheet metal, which was why it would
cost $150 to have a 6¢ heater control replaced by the Chrysler
garage. And why it had cost Harold a day and a half to do it himself
the year before.

Harold unbolted the front and rear seats and put them in the
yard, which is where Ethel saw them on her way to the compost
heap. "I hope you aren't planning to leave those things there."

"No. Leave good seats like that outdoors? These are destined
for the living room," Harold said. "I'm gonna mount them on a
two-by-four frame. They're a little unstable now."

"It's not like you to give me straight lines," Ethel said.

*　　*　　*　　　*　　　*　　*　　　*　　　*　　*　　*

9

HAROLD USED HIS TRACTOR AND LOADER TO PULL
the engine block and transmission out of the Blue Bomber today
in 1987. In the winter he would take the automatic transmission
apart and study it. It would be good entertainment and educational.

Harold removed the trunk lid from the old Chrysler and stored
it with the hood. He took off all four wheels. And then Harold
began filling the engine area and the trunk and the passenger
compartment with topsoil hauled in from the field.

Ethel came out and said, "What are you doing?"

"It's gonna be a 1970 Chrysler hotbed and greenhouse. Pe-
rennials in the trunk and under the hood, and tomatoes and that
sort of stuff in the main cabin. I can adjust the temperature by
cranking the windows up and down. It's the best idea I've had in
ten years."

"I'd hate to tell you how many people would agree."

*　　*　　*　　　*　　　*　　*　　　*　　　*　　*　　*

10

ON THIS DAY IN 1986 PHIL DANFORTH HAD A ribbon-cutting ceremony at his farm near Fulda, Minnesota, to celebrate the construction of his new custom-built wind generator and sixty-foot tower. He delivered a few emotion-packed words about how he would not only be self-sufficient energy-wise but he would also be selling spare electricity to the power company. Holding back the tears of joy, he went on to say how proud he was to live in the windiest part of the whole nation and in the windiest part of the windiest state, and rather than cuss the wind as so many people did, he was embracing it. He pulled the switch to start the system.

* * * * * * * * *

11

ON THIS DAY IN 1986 PHIL DANFORTH WAS UP IN the dark, walking from room to room in the farmhouse, turning lights on and off. He woke the family to tell them it was a gift from heaven. He was tired but happy all day. He developed a little vertigo from watching the blades go around on the generator.

* * * * * * * * *

12

THE BIG WEATHER FRONT THEY HAD BEEN TALKING about on the news the night before did roll into Phil Danforth's area this day in 1986. It was the ultimate test. The lights powered by the generator lit up the darkness of the storm right up until the time the high winds buckled the tower. It fell on the empty ten-thousand-bushel grain bin, turning it into a five-hundred-bushel grain bin with an unhandy door. It also reduced Phil Danforth's Chrysler LeBaron to a thin slab of maroon-colored steel with tilt, cruise, and air. Phil thought it could be worse, but he would have to think a while to decide how.

* * * * * * * * *

13

THIS IS ALWAYS THE DAY LAWRENCE NIVAG SHUTS down the oil furnace and closes the valve to the barrel to end the heating season at his home in Fineview. It is also the day he always takes his income-tax return to the post office so he can drop it in the mail and miss the rush and have more time to complain to the postmaster about the feds.

Lawrence refuses to turn the furnace back on until October 15. If April happens to be chilly and there is frost every morning in the low-lying areas, Lawrence still won't budge. His wife, Patricia, has asked to have the furnace turned back on in May, for instance, when one of those cold Canadian clippers rolled across the state and she was in the living room with her coat on and her fingers turning blue. But Lawrence always delivers the same speech: "It's not healthy and it's against my principles. I don't eat oatmeal with raisins in it because it looks like something from the pasture, I don't drive on the highways after eleven at night, I don't wear colored underwear, and I don't turn on the furnace after I've turned it off at the appropriate time." In some marriages this would be grounds for divorce, but the fact is that Lawrence has plenty of good points to recommend him; his Gestapo furnace policy is not one of them.

*   *   *   *   *   *   *   *   *   *

14

TIMELY INCOME-TAX TIPS FOR CAT OWNERS: CAN a cat be used as a medical deduction? Yes and no. If it's an over-the-counter cat, probably not. But if your physician prescribed a cat for you, or you purchased it through an HMO, it is a legal deduction under the "medicinal-cat" ruling of 1984.

In another ruling, however, the IRS maintains that the cost of feeding your cat is not an "entertainment" expense: a cat entertains when and if it feels like it, not because you feed it.

A litter of kittens is considered capital gains if you sell them, but the tax burden can be shared with the owner of the tomcat if you can find him.

*   *   *   *   *   *   *   *   *   *

15

This day brought to you by BACKYARD TAX SHELTERS, the backyard solution to your tax problems. If these are your prime earning years and you want a tax-free roof over your loose change, call the BACKYARD TAX SHELTERS people and have them build one to your specs. When those big companies take your money and manage it, you don't have any idea where it is. *IT COULD BE ANY-WHERE!!!!* EVEN IN THEIR POCKETS!!!! And if you ask to see it, they act like you just got off the boat.

When you put your money in a quality-built BACKYARD TAX SHELTER, you'll know exactly where it is, and you have a choice of several popular styles, including Victorian, Greek, Art Deco, and Cheap. BACKYARD TAX SHELTERS are for people who want their surplus cash to flow into the backyard, where they can get their hands on it and count it once in a while to see if it's all there.

And every darn penny you put in your BACKYARD TAX SHELTER will be exempt from taxes. It's the law, signed by the President. He's got a couple of BACKYARD TAX SHELTERS himself: a Neo-Gothic out beyond the helicopter pad and a Natural Cedar Ranch-Rustic at Camp David.

*   *   *   *   *   *   *   *   *   *

16

ON THIS DAY IN 1950 HAROLD MIRE'S GRANDFATHER decided that an eleven-year-old boy ought to be playing baseball not listening to the radio, so he gave Harold a children's-model fielder's glove that he bought at a toy store. It looked like a swollen Ping-Pong paddle without a handle. You could spit and punch all day and not get a pocket in it. Harold took it to school like a doomed kid and in Phys Ed he was chosen last and stood in right field only this one time with the leather albatross on the end of his arm and the only ball that came his way bounced off of it and struck him on the cheekbone.

After school he went home and buried the glove in the back-yard, next to the orange puckered nylon shirt his grandma had given him for Christmas. Then he went into his room and listened to "Jack Armstrong, the All-American Boy" and read *Popular Mechanics*.

*   *   *   *   *   *   *   *   *   *

17

ON THIS DAY IN 1987 HAROLD MIRE ANNOUNCED one of a subset of rules to his daughter, who had just got her driver's license. She could hear Lecture No. 9 coming up: "Always assume that every other vehicle on the road has a bozo behind the wheel who will make every mistake possible. You should act accordingly."

The phone rang and she left for school and never heard the rest of No. 9, which wasn't his worst one. That would be either Lecture No. 3 ("Planning a Little") or No. 8 ("Sugared Cereals"). It wasn't that she disagreed with him necessarily, or thought his presentations lacked wit and charm—it was just that they suffered greatly from endless repetition. But since she was the child and he was the parent, she didn't exactly know how to tell him this without hurting his feelings.

*   *   *   *   *   *   *   *   *   *

18

ON THIS DAY IN 1988 THE NEW EXHIBIT IN THE Primate Wing at the Zoo was closed by the Humane Society. On April 17 the curators had captured forty-two Minnesota poets without a struggle and put them behind glass at a realistic wine-and-cheese party in a small apartment. The Humane Society said that even though the poets seemed to be having fun, the air in the exhibit was worse than the conversation and hazardous to the health.

*   *   *   *   *   *   *   *   *   *

19

THIS EVENING IN 1988 MINNESOTA BIGFOOT WAS not sighted and barely heard as a guest on a radio program called

"The *Titanic*." He didn't know the words to "Nearer My God to Thee," but he gamely held hands with the cast and hummed along on the theme song.

* * * * * * * * * *

20

ON THIS DAY IN 1979 THE HEAD HONCHOS AT HARE Krishna headquarters discovered that its missionaries in Minnesota were approaching people and saying, "I guess if you want to make a donation you can but you don't have to. Whatever. It's no big deal. Take this mint anyway."

In an action heard later by the Court of Religious Appeals, the attorneys for the Hare Krishna church claimed that Minnesota was a cult engaged in brainwashing the innocent and well-meaning disciples. They presented in evidence the fact that nine out of ten Hare Krishna true believers refused to obey their leaders after just a week in the Gopher State and spent a lot of time walleye-fishing.

The judge ruled that even if they converted to Lutheranism while here, it would do very little harm, in his opinion.

* * * * * * * * * *

21

THIS IS THE DAY MINNESOTA GOES ON SEASON Savings Time. Simply turn your calendar back one month, to March 21, unless you live in Goodhue County, which does not participate. In Wright County wait until April 25. And of course on September 30 don't forget to flip your calendar forward to October 30. Remember: Spring Behind and Fall Forward to Winter. If your birthday occurs within the repeated New Spring days, celebrate all you want but advance only one year; the house payments and Visa bill should be paid both times. The IRS should be paid only once, on whichever April 15 suits you, but the Minnesota Commissioner of Revenue wants your taxes twice.

One more note: the period between September 30 and October 30 does not exist under Season Savings Time. This will probably make you feel real tired until way after Christmas, but if you can hang on until April 21, you can sleep for a month and catch up.

* * * * * * * * * *

22

ON THIS DAY IN 1987 THE MINNESOTA AG INSTITUTE published the *Catalog of Modern Farming Styles and Personalities*. The following excerpts are reprinted by permission:

"Chuck Yeager": These farmers stretch the envelope of planting and harvest by going as fast as possible and then pushing it a little more, and are distinguished by their jet-assisted tractors and turbo pickups. They can be recognized at the implement dealer's counter by their leather flight jackets, aviator glasses, and insatiable need for repair parts. Farming for them is the moral equivalent of war.

"Wall Street": These farmers take a late breakfast, read the paper in their robes, do fieldwork from 9:00 until 12:00, take a long dinner, do field work from 1:30 to 3:00, and then shower and sit on the deck in their smoking jackets, or go shoot a round of golf and have a nightcap at the clubhouse for some serious complaining.

"Gentleman Farmer": The guy works in town but lives on ten acres or less tillable, and farms it as if he invented agriculture. He generally owns $10,000 worth of new equipment per acre and his cost of growing a crop is at least twice what he earns from it. He believes in doing it right. He often has to take a second job in town to help support his avant-garde farming methods. His wife already works.

"Back a Notch": These farmers go as fast as they dare and then drop it back a notch. They get as much done as the "Chuck Yeagers" because they spend on the average two hours less a day repairing equipment, but they don't wear sunglasses or leather jackets. Farming for them is the moral equivalent of a police action.

"Gospel": These farmers know that many that are first shall be last; and the last shall be first. They also know that it's a good idea to grease the bearings every two hours and fix it before it's broke.

"Kamikaze": These farmers operate on a simple philosophy: If it ain't broke, break it.

"Glacier": These farmers are always in low gear, always throttled back—it may take them up to a day to cross the field once. They often finish planting as harvest begins, so there's never a dull moment.

"Baling Wire": These farmers believe that farming's main purpose is to keep old equipment in operating condition by improvising repairs. Chances are when you drive by their place, they'll be in the yard with the welder. On the average they spend eight hours repairing and two hours farming each day. But they save a lot of money and seem to be about as happy as the *"Glaciers."*

"Secretive": These farmers work at night and are rarely seen during the day. Their skin is pale, their eyes large. Nobody knows how they keep their rows straight in the dark and nobody wants to ask.

"Arthur Godfrey": These farmers are equipped with the latest FM two-way radios in all their vehicles and have tall transmitting towers at the home base: they go on the air at dawn and entertain three counties with their daily variety show. Not recommended for children.

*   *   *   *   *   *   *   *   *   *

23

THIS WOULD BE A GOOD DAY FOR YOU TO CHECK your house for sharp corners you could bump your head on, like the table, the edge of the piano there, those heavy stereo speakers you thought you had to have, the medicine cabinet sticking out above the sink, and that ridiculously overpriced antique pie-case in the living room. That's for starters. Take a survey before it's too late. Folded newspapers about four inches by four inches and a half-inch thick, shaped to fit the menacing corners and held down with packing tape, works fairly well.

*   *   *   *   *   *   *   *   *   *

24

WHEN HAROLD MIRE'S DAUGHTER CAME HOME from high school on this day in 1987 he asked her how it went. She said, "I survived."

Harold heard himself say, "These are the best years of your life." He was about to say that you're only young once, but Lily was already looking up to heaven for deliverance, so he skipped it; besides Harold realized that he was saying exactly what his folks used to tell him.

But was it true? This was the question. He hadn't thought so when he was a teenager, but now that he was an almost fully functional adult, he wanted to test the premise before he got himself into any more pontificating.

If his school days had been the best years of his life, the graduation ceremony in 1956 would not be among the supporting data. Everybody else had a good time and his mother had the photos to prove it in the cedar chest. His relatives had crawled out of the walls for it and showered him with billfolds and undershirts and pencil sets and anywhere from $2 to $5 inside quilted cards with embossed messages.

What Harold recalled was walking up on the stage at the end of the gymnasium and having the superintendent shake his hand and say, "Hurgghh Merrr, forest mushes musdit, browsss theno!!! Aagitendo, lumph." It was easy for him to say. And Harold had managed a sick smile in return and marched down the steps on the other side of the stage and down along the lunchroom-counter side of the crowd, where he was met by flashbulbs wielded by his family.

*   *   *   *   *   *   *   *   *   *

25

HAROLD WOKE UP ON THIS DAY IN 1987 WORKING hard to come up with two or three bell-ringers that had contributed to the best years of his life. It *wasn't* the time he rode with Eddie Carver to the basketball game in that black Mercury of his and

Eddie lost it on the Benson curve trying to do what he called a four-wheel power drift. Whatever it was, he didn't do it right, unless Harold was supposed to hit his forehead on the rearview mirror when they bounced into the ditch and came up on two wheels. Harold still had the scar above his right eye. Wiping out on the Benson curve made a good story with the guys at school, but in 1987 Harold could only think how stupid he was to ride with that maniac.

When his daughter got home from school he would tell her not to ride with Eddie Carver—he would be sporting ducktails and chain-smoking Old Golds.

* * *   *   *   *   *   *   *   *

26

AS HAROLD MIRE WAS GOING OUT THE DOOR HE remembered the time the fourth-grade teacher caught him looking up "whore" in the H section of the dictionary and pulled his ear and made him sit up front for having a dirty mind after he told her what word he was looking for. That was the end of Harold's innocence and the beginning of his improvement in spelling.

* * *   *   *   *   *   *   *

27

IN HIS SEARCH THROUGH THE BEST YEARS OF HIS life Harold took a look back at Fremson High's old basketball court, where he had begun his basketball career, before the new gym and stage and hot-lunch room were built.

The old gym was a sunken box with no windows and one door located three feet from the boundary line. The spectators watched from a railing above. The brick walls behind the baskets were hung with old mattresses. The standards were fastened to the wall—the distance between the out-of-bounds line and the wall was fifteen inches. If you had a big butt you didn't get to take the ball out under the basket.

But the best years of Harold's life didn't seem to include the time in the old gym during a game with Beeman when he was rear-

ended by six players after he made a sudden stop during a fast
break to avoid hitting the door after Tiny Holmes opened it. It
seemed funny now, but then it had been humiliating. The crowd
loved it—all they had needed was a lion to come out and eat the
players and they could go home satisfied. Three of the Beeman
players got rear-ending fouls called on them, but Harold missed
all six shots—the number of shots had been decided by a special
ruling from the referee, who said the books didn't cover it. It was
the biggest pile-up in league history and the most foul shots taken
by one player in sequence and the most missed.

*   *   *   *   *   *   *   *   *   *

28 HAROLD MUST HAVE DREAMED ABOUT THE BEST
years of his life because he woke up this morning in 1987 with
news: it could be when he got to be sixty years old his school days
would become the best years of his life. He would take a wait-and-
see position.

And at that moment he thought of something: the trip to Pendleton with the junior class and what's his name, the superintendent . . . Mr. Bosco. Pendleton was where the insane asylum was—
that's what people called it. When somebody was "up at Pendleton"
they weren't on vacation. They were crazy.

That's what Harold had thought too. But that was before he
got off the school bus and went into the locked ward on the second
floor and sat with a few Pendleton residents, all adults. They
wanted to talk and they wanted to know how his life was going,
and they wanted to play checkers. He made them laugh and they
made him laugh. And they didn't want him to go when Mr. Bosco
gave the call, and Harold didn't want to leave. He had no idea
why those people were there, but it was obvious to him that they
were his compatriots. The sort of people who would stick by you
through thick and thin. Pals. If he ever needed a place to go, he
had said to himself, he'd go to Pendleton.

So there it was, finally, one thing that had made Harold's school
days the best years of his life. There had to be more days like that
if he kept dredging.

But it *wasn't* the time in third grade, after school, when the

principal thought it was Harold who had yelled in the hall and
shook him so hard he wet his pants—three splotches in the front
and down the whole right leg to the cuff. He had seven blocks to
walk home and it took him over an hour, what with avoiding the
sidewalks and taking people's lawns and hiding in the bushes.

*   *   *   *   *   *   *   *   *   *

29

ON THIS OPENING DAY OF CANTERBURY DOWNS IN
1988 Minnesota Bigfoot was sighted making a bet that was below
the average wager needed for the horsetrack to break even, according to management. The track accountants asked him to leave
for not doing his fair share, but they didn't press the issue. Bigfoot
went on to parlay his two bucks into thirty, which wasn't too bad
for a large, hairy primate who had spent most of his life alone in
the north woods.

*   *   *   *   *   *   *   *   *   *

30

ON THIS DAY IN 1978 THE HOLY ALTERNATIVE
Carpenter Brothers opened their tent for business and were immediately asked to remodel a house for Minnesota's reigning queen
of natural rhyme, Wilma Klog, whose last work had been written
entirely with a sharpened stone on a cave wall. Wilma did not
believe in technology, which was why she hired Roy and Basil to
remove all modern conveniences from her house, including nails,
and fix up a few holes.

Roy and Basil were just the ticket because they owned no power
tools; they fastened things together with rawhide or hemp. And if
they had to shorten a board so it didn't stick out, they either broke
it off by jumping on it, or used a saw made from buffalo bones.
This was as pure as carpentry ever got.

When the Holy Alternative Carpenter Brothers were finished
with Wilma's house, in 1982, it looked like a clump of humus with
a chimney, which was exactly what she'd had in mind, she said in

the beautiful couplets of the commemorative poem she presented to her carpenters in lieu of cash, which she felt was dirty. Roy and Basil also expressed their feelings about cash, but without rhyming it. They decided to ask for a contract on their next project and also file some teeth in their buffalo saw.

*   *   *   *   *   *   *   *   *

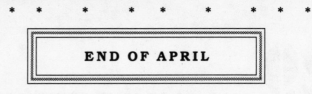

END OF APRIL

MAY

1 TODAY IS THE BEGINNING OF THE WOOD-TICK SEASON in Minnesota. The Wood Tick Control Center reminds you that you are now under a Wood Tick Watch until further notice. A watch means that the threat of wood ticks exists and a wood tick could crawl up your leg at any time. A Wood Tick Warning means that the Color Wood Tick Radar at Control Center has detected a band of wood ticks on somebody's clothes or hair, or inside socks and boots and ears, in the Warning Area. If you are in the Warning Area, tune to your local station, take cover, remove your clothes, and check yourself from head to toe for wood ticks. If you find a wood tick burrowed into your scalp or any other part of your person, remember this rhyme:

Don't pull it out with pliers
Just cover it with Vaseline
Until it expires.

Send for your copy of the free pamphlet from the Wood Tick Control Center: *Where to Look for Wood Ticks on Yourself or Anybody Else.*

* * * * * * * * * *

2 **This day and the several that follow are sponsored by GODWIN GABBERT,** better known as "MR. VEGETABLE" to thousands of fans who hear his gardening call-in show every week on Gopher State Radio. MR. VEGETABLE will answer some of the frequent gardening questions he receives from his listeners.

Q: How much should I plant, Mr. Vegetable?

Mr. V: You have planted too much if by early August your friends have already started pulling their shades down and turning off the lights when you come up the sidewalk with a big grin and several full baskets of produce whose proportions are wrong.

* * * * * * * * * *

3

Today is made possible by "GABBERT'S GARDEN."

Q: Are those novelty vegetables a good idea, Mr. Vegetable?

MR. V: Never plant seeds for vegetables that look on the package like they will end up weighing more than you do, whatever that is. These generally taste like polyester and could injure you if they shift unexpectedly.

*   *   *   *   *   *   *   *   *   *   *

4

Another tough question for today's sponsor.

Q: Are rutabagas very hard to grow, Mr. Vegetable?

MR. V: A child could do it, but the problem is their only known use is in a Central American contact sport that also involves a two-pointed stick and plastic eyebrows.

*   *   *   *   *   *   *   *   *   *   *

GODWIN GABBERT, today's sponsor, does not pull punches.

Q: Can okra be grown in Minnesota, Mr. Vegetable?

MR. V: I'm sorry to say it can, but pick it when it's small and never boil it unless you are short on nasal mucus for the doorknob. If the pods get longer than three inches they make good firewood.

*   *   *   *   *   *   *   *   *   *   *

6

Today's sponsor sometimes steps over the bounds of good taste.

Q: What animals will be interested in my garden, Mr. Vegetable?

Mr. V: It would be easier to say which won't be. The following animals are already making plans today to enter your garden: rabbits, raccoons, deer, pocket gophers, mice, moles, groundhogs, chickens, horses, goats, sheep, cows, pigs, dogs, and children. Try to keep them out.

Raccoons are a major sweet-corn predator and will always attack the sweet corn the night before the day you thought you'd pick it. To prevent this, wrap a portable radio in a Baggie and place it in the patch. Raccoons are especially repelled by Lite Rock.

The cheapest way to keep rabbits out of your garden is to urinate up and down the rows next to the vegetables, but this has a built-in male bias and can lead to rumors and arrest in urban areas. Carry it out in a sprinkler.

*   *   *   *   *   *   *   *   *   *

7

Mr. Vegetable reminds you to tune in to "GABBERT'S GARDEN" on Gopher State Radio every Saturday morning, right after "Dr. Cure Me."

Q: When I try to talk about gardening, people rush from the room, Mr. Vegetable—what could it be?

Mr. V: Two people in love are infinitely appealing to each other, but one person in love with a garden is another story. If you are a passionate gardener, remember that mulching is not nearly the thrill for others it is for you. Tilling and telling is bad manners.

*   *   *   *   *   *   *   *   *   *

8

ON THIS DAY IN 1976 DON LARRY WAS CAPTURED by a bratwurst-shaped flying saucer and later dropped off at a fishing-lure factory near Owatonna, Minnesota, with small electrical burns on his earlobes, a big pimple on the end of his nose, and no elastic in his beltless trousers.

*   *   *   *   *   *   *   *   *   *

9

ON THIS DAY IN 1987 BUSTER AIRLINES BECAME THE first domestic air carrier to have the restrictions that applied on its cheap flights reach the best-seller list. The following advertisement appeared in several Minnesota newspapers in 1987 and is reprinted by permission of the publisher.

☞ SOME RESTRICTIONS DO APPLY**!!!

An instant bestseller!!!
341 big, big pages of tiny, tiny print!!!
*You get all 7573 restrictions that do apply!!** on the $24.95 Go*
*   *Anywhere Cheap fare from Buster Airlines!!!*
Including:

*You must fly between one a.m. and four a.m. on the second even-numbered Saturday of each month unless it is a holiday weekend.

*A holiday weekend is defined as any weekend that occurs seven days before or after a holiday.

*A holiday is defined as any holiday celebrated nationally or a holiday celebrated locally in the destination or departure state or city.

*For example: If you fly to Marshalltown, Iowa, within seven days of Corn Cob Day, our $24.49 fare would not be available. Corn Cob Day is celebrated sometime between June 17 and August 2, depending on the weather.

*For example: Buster Airlines President Myron Mochamp's birthday on May 12 is considered a national holiday. Myron and Sweetie's anniversary is no longer a holiday since the divorce.

*Reservations must be made two years in advance.

*On round trips you must fly home the same direction you came. For example: if you fly from Cleveland to Kansas City, you must return to Cleveland by flying west.

*You must appear at the airport at least forty-eight hours before your flight. Camping available.

*Bring your own sleeping bag and tent to the Go Anywhere Cheap barbwire compound behind the charter terminal.

*Buster Airlines reserves the right to bump you back home for up to ten days if a customer with more money willing to pay the regular fare shows up before the flight attendants put their gum behind their ears and test the microphones.

*Your bottom cushion cannot be used as a flotation device.

*You may be required to share your seat with another Go Anywhere Cheap passenger of the same sex or religious affiliation.

*Your seat back must be brought forward at all times.

*Carry-on luggage restricted to one thirteen-gallon plastic garbage bag with twist tie.

*You will be required to do light housekeeping duties in the galley.

*At remote airports you may be asked to remove dead birds from the turbines.

All that and much, much more when you buy:

Some Restrictions Do Apply

At a bookstore near you!!!!

Or call Daryl at Buster Airlines and he'll ship you a copy out. Be sure to let it ring a few times—it takes Daryl a while to climb the stairs from the boiler room, although he's a lot faster since his leg healed and he started taking medication for his wheezing.

*   *   *   *   *   *   *   *   *   *

10

ON THIS DAY IN 1979 KYLE AND TRUDY MIFTE OF rural Granite Falls stripped the bedding from their queen-size bed and decided to turn the motel-quality foam mattress over and use the other side for a while. The mattress emitted a sigh and a cloud of yellow dust that was the product of fifteen years of hard sleeping and mature tossing and turning from two people who weren't getting any smaller. Kyle lugged the mattress out to the trash-burner area and set it on fire. When his neighbor drove up to check on the thick smoke, Kyle told him he was just burning their bed, and then realized too late that this remark would be repeated, with elaborations, several times by the many gifted storytellers who had nothing better to do.

*   *   *   *   *   *   *   *   *   *

11

This day brought to you by HOUSEHOLD ODORIZER of St. Cloud, the custom-made scent that smells like home.

V. Duckworth of Edina says: "I used to get so lonely and depressed on sales trips. And sometimes even down at the office I'd get a little low. But that never happens now that I carry HOUSEHOLD ODORIZER. With a couple shots of H.O. I make wherever I am smell just like home. My home. Sometimes I even use it in cabs on my way back and forth from the airport, or I release a burst into the conference room before a presentation."

To receive your custom-made odor, send us an air sample from your house and label it clearly.

Minnesota snowbirds Gretta and Max Neunber say: "We never head for Phoenix without a can of our personal household odor from H.O. It makes our trailer home in the desert smell exactly like 2456 Murchison Court North. And for some reason it keeps the scorpions out, too."

For the budget-minded, HOUSEHOLD ODORIZER is available over-the-counter in popular generic odors, including Liver & Onions, Wet Dog, Fried Potatoes, Farmhouse Porch, Stale Beer, Litter Box, Wood Stove, and Chain Smoker. Buy several odors and experiment until you get the atmosphere you desire. Look for it in the can with the flared nostrils painted on the side.

(Sorry: No refunds on custom odor orders.)

*   *   *   *   *   *   *   *   *   *

12

ALL THE FRIENDS OF RICK SHERMAN WHO HAD BEEN sending him family letters at Christmas over the years would soon receive their first and only Xeroxed Christmas letter from Rick soon after this day in 1986, when he mailed fifty-seven copies.

Greetings.

I can't express adequately in words or happy faces in the margins how much I have appreciated the family letters sent over the long haul of years. It was great, getting a whole year's news of your ups and downs. The ups were inspiring and very tastefully presented and with very little of that crowing and tooting of one's own horn sometimes produced by family-oriented egotists who think the universe revolves around them and their homes.

As you know, I keep a tight rein on my emotions, but I feel close to you right now and won't try to hide my disappointments, because you so often made them the center of your Christmas letters when it was a rough year. Sometimes it was hard to believe how every year you could be involved in so many unusual and fresh domestic disasters.

The biggest change in your Christmas letters came in the early 1980s when many of you started buying entry-level personal computers with primitive word-processing and cheesy dot-matrix printers. But when you upgraded, I was amazed by how you were able to change typefaces and size from paragraph to paragraph—and even from sentence to sentence!! It jazzed up your prose immensely. And the computer-drawn pictures you used to enhance your messages—well, I was dumfounded.

But more than anything I have felt guilty reading your annual letters. There you were spilling your heart out year after year in incredible detail and here I was sitting like a lump and a voyeur. I meant to correct that imbalance by composing a

Christmas letter that would be a classic of bowl reading; I
envisioned it sitting on the top of your toilet tank, where you
would plow through it chapter by chapter, whenever the urge
struck you. But one thing led to another and as you can see I
didn't even get this thing mailed by Christmas. Please feel free
to flesh it out as you see fit.

☞ PREFACE

Star (Nova???). Wisemen. Manger. Peace on earth. Good
will, etc.
Holly.
Grandma's house, through the woods, over hill and dale, big
bad wolf.
Sleigh bells ringing, ding-a-ling.
Also chestnuts roasting on an open fire.
Discount stores, blue-light specials.
Carts full of toys based on Saturday-morning cartoons.
Burglaries by men dressed like Santa.
But nevertheless, it's Christmas, and who can escape the
holiday spirit? Not me.
Wish it seemed like only yesterday took pen in hand.

☞ DISEASES

Overview. Dow Jones–style graphs of sickness and health
for each family member, line graph for family as whole.
Explanation of disease peak in '81 with measles, mumps,
rash (it was our soap), gas (it was our water), ear infections,
and irritability (it was our blood sugar).
Disease valley in '83 with no diagnosable diseases but a lot
of complaining and fruitless trips to the clinic. Doctors said it
was in our head or was nonspecific colitis—something you people are very familiar with, as I recall.
Humorous side effects of prescription drugs.

☞CHILDREN

Conception information: hammock, rooftop, tornado.
Birth stories.
First words. Cute sayings. Precocious behavior and insight. Reading at two years. Composing verse at three.
Toilet training, child by child. Last was hardest: Newspapers spread on floor in corner and then rolled up and used for tapping on head. Reward system. Litter box. Why us?
K–12, by years, by child. Photocopies of report cards, school papers.
Braces. Saving bundle by changing to orthodontist who drove Toyota instead of Jaguar.

☞FAMILY TRIPS

International Falls, Fort Frances, tour of Boise Cascade paper mill. Odor. Noise.
Wisconsin Dells. Meant to go to Black Hills, took wrong turn. Couldn't see much difference except no faces of presidents. Plenty of gewgaws.
At the cabin, by years, including '79 invasion of fire ants and brown recluse spiders, '73 boat rot, '82 Moonies bought cabin next to ours. Chart of yearly catches of walleye, northern, crappies, bluegills, sunnies.
San Diego. People eating tiny ice-cream cones. Houses built on hillsides. No visible work being done.

☞HOUSE DISASTERS

Insulated walls of house for energy efficiency.
Took out insulation in walls because it had formaldehyde in it.
Finished the basement, ceiling tile.
Removed asbestos ceiling tile.
Removed finished basement walls when block foundation gave way.
Paid for house twice over, still had same house.
Put on family room east side of house. Entertainment center a foot over property line. Neighbor makes us move it in and

*then puts up one-quarter-inch steel fence to contain their llamas
and poodles and secret life.*

*Roof trusses popping like mousetraps, total mystery to con-
tractor.*

Replacement of trusses during rainy week.

Piper Cub landing on garage.

☞ OTHER

How tired we felt during each year, charted.

How old we felt, year by year, charted.

Home-appliance adventures.

*How it could have been worse, year by year, charted. In
1978 it couldn't have been worse, because that was the worst
year we had as a family.*

☞ CONCLUSION

*Anyway, a heartfelt though belated Merry Christmas and
Happy New Year to each and every one of you. And as long
as I've got my good cheer up to speed, have a great summer.*

I better wind this up while my eyes are still dry.

Yours,

Rick and family.

*   *   *   *   *   *   *   *   *   *

13

HAROLD MIRE REACHED NEW HEIGHTS IN HIS
handling of door-to-door salesmen on this day in 1987. His policy
for the hawkers who drove into his yard had always been simple:
the salesman would say, "Well, Mr. Mire, I'm sure you are interested in the education of your children," for example, and Harold
would say, "I never buy anything from salesmen who come to my
door."

Today though, Harold added something: "Listen, if you've got
a second, you look like a gentleman that is handy with tools. I've
got just what you're looking for." Harold then brought out the
sample case of tools he had bought at the hardware store. The

young man working himself through college while driving a Cadillac had not been presented with this possibility at the sales school in Tennessee, so he weakened and looked. Harold turned up the heat.

When the salesman walked back to his Eldorado, he was carrying a screwdriver set that Harold had let him have at $12.95, exactly $4 more than Harold had paid for it. Not a bad day's work for an amateur.

*   *   *   *   *   *   *   *   *   *

14

ON THIS FISHING-OPENER DAY IN 1988 JERRY Bjornson pulled his van up the driveway of Ernie's house in Woodbury at a little before 4:00 A.M. Howard and Ernie were bivouacked on the lawn, smoking cigars. They figured they'd be on Rice Lake by 6:15 at the latest. It went like clockwork.

4:11 Departure delayed while Jerry takes off air cleaner, fiddles with automatic choke. Backfiring wakes neighborhood.

4:18 I-494. Hint of dawn. Passing a darkened Taco Village. Ernie excited about new fish-finder with hi-res screen.

4:27 Passing Taco Village again. Still darkened. Fish-finder inside the garage door. Blame each other.

5:09 Siren, flashing lights.

5:20 Highway Patrol officer wishes them good luck. Writes ticket for faulty taillights on boat trailer.

5:45 Taping, twisting of wire proceeds until sky bright enough so taillights superfluous. Renewed hope. New day. Climb every mountain, fish every lake.

5:45 Jerry sure as hell glad got bigger engine in van. Hardly tell pulling anything. Howard looks side mirror. Good news, pulling trailer. Bad news, no boat on it.

5:59 Find boat sitting in gravel, rest area. Restraining straps beside boat. Blame each other.

7:30 Boat in waters of Rice Lake. Howard in waters of Rice Lake. Slipped, pushing. Face down. Soaks Cuban cigars.

7:36 Howard hooks Jerry's lucky fishing hat on cast. Large northern strikes hat, snaps line, dives. Hat sinks.

7:54 Ernie sidesteps spilled night-crawlers, knocks ham, cheese sandwiches into water. Eaten by cruising carp.

8:34 Move more toward point with crooked pine tree.

8:39 Deeper than looks. Jerry drops anchor. Keeps going. Rope unattached. Blame each other. Trolling begins. Best anyway.

8:41 Ernie thinks fish-finder not working, electromagnetic fields in stern, trips on landing net on way to bow. Fish-finder arches up, out of boat.

8:42 Ernie chosen to dive for fish-finder.

9:37 Ernie finds fish-finder, water sloshing inside advanced solid-state circuitry.

6:52 Decide make it even twelve hours without fish.

7:30 Done. Never say die.

8:00 Inside Serendipity Supper Club, specialty walleye. Ernie, Howard, Jerry order prime rib. Cool center, still quivering. This the life.

11:15 Siren behind van.

11:17 Second ticket. Same trailer light. Blame each other.

11:53 Jerry fiddles with automatic choke in Ernie's driveway. Backfire wakes neighborhood.

11:59 Agree can't say wasn't fun.

* * * * * * * * * *

15

MINNESOTA BIGFOOT WAS SIGHTED ON THIS DAY IN 1987 talking on the LoveLine for only 59¢ a minute. He had seen how much fun the young men and women were having in the advertisement the night before during the Charlie Chan movie. Bigfoot's natural shyness and throaty grunts got him invitations to

three parties and some other stuff he didn't understand and didn't
want to.

*   *   *   *   *   *   *   *   *   *

16

ON THIS DAY IN 1988 TWO DAYS AFTER THE FISHING
opener, Mack R. Hanson published a Minnesota business strategy
book called *Battle with the Bullheads Without Having the Greasy
Slime Rub Off—Outbull, Outpull, Outscavenge the Bottom Feed-
ers.* Over three thousand people attended his lecture at the St. Paul
Civic Center thinking they would learn some techniques of bullhead fishing, but when they discovered it was only another ghostwritten book about profits, they got up and walked out.

*   *   *   *   *   *   *   *   *   *

17

ON THIS DAY IN 1988 D. PETERS PUBLISHED A
business-strategy book called *Awash with the Walleyes—Wallow-
ing with the Worst.* It immediately went to the top of the "Business
Books with Fish in the Title" Best-Seller List.

*   *   *   *   *   *   *   *   *   *

18

ON THIS DAY IN 1988 MINNESOTAN BOB E. DOBBETS
published a business-strategy book called *Contending with the
Carp Without Exactly Becoming a Carp or Necessarily Scavenging
and Growing in Water That Would Gag a Maggot.*

*   *   *   *   *   *   *   *   *   *

19

ON THIS DAY IN 1988 SARAH TONNINGS PUBLISHED
Mixing with the Minnows Without Being Netted by the Guys Who

*Make a Living Selling Bait or Being Taken to Lunch by All the
Bigger Fish.*

*   *   *   *   *   *   *   *   *   *

20

ON THIS DAY IN 1988 NO BUSINESS-STRATEGY BOOK
was published by a Minnesotan, but three new ones were started.

*   *   *   *   *   *   *   *   *   *

21

WITH SOME MONEY HER AUNT SENT HER FOR HER
birthday, Lily Mire, age seventeen, bought herself a compound
bow and a half-dozen wooden arrows at a sporting-goods store today
in 1988 and proceeded to practice on a few bales of hay in the
yard. Harold came home from helping a friend move a new stove
and asked what the deal was, operating a lethal weapon and all.

"It's exercise," Lily said. "Archery is a sport."

Harold said, "Volleyball is a sport. Have you ever heard of a
war fought with volleyballs?"

"No," Lily said, "but if I thought I had any say in the matter,
that's the kind of war I would prefer." Harold couldn't think of a
reply right then.

*   *   *   *   *   *   *   *   *   *

22

ON THIS EVENING IN 1986 HAROLD AND ETHEL
were sitting and talking on the couch in the living room waiting
for the ten o'clock news on Channel 5 to end so they could get the
forecast. They were toting things up, something they had begun
doing more of lately. Bowls of oatmeal consumed in a lifetime, for
instance. Tonight they estimated they had slept together in the
same double bed in that tiny back bedroom for nearly twenty years,
over seven thousand nights. As soon as the weather news was done,
they went in there and continued the march toward eight thousand.
What alternatives did they have?

*   *   *   *   *   *   *   *   *   *

23

ON THIS DAY IN 1986 HAROLD MIRE WENT IN FOR his six-week haircut and told his barber of seventeen years, Mr. Kris, to take a little more off than last time, which had been a light trim so he didn't look scalped for his niece's confirmation. He guessed he wanted a heavy trim or a medium cut maybe. In his opinion it was too long in the back now. Mr. Kris told him to relax, he knew exactly what to do. As he finished, he told Harold he wanted to try something new he had read in *The Barber's Edge*.

"I want to make your left sideburn longer than the right, because the effect'll be to improve the appearance of your ear placement, which is afflicted with a bilateral anomaly, the left ear being an inch and a half lower than the right."

"That's too modern for me," Harold said. "Let's just leave my ears squeehunky, the way God intended. I'm not in a beauty contest."

*   *   *   *   *   *   *   *   *   *

24

HISTORY WAS MADE THIS PROM NIGHT IN 1987 AT the Boxelder High School, when four couples arrived in a chauffeured stretch Ford pickup from Lloyd's Class Cartage. Sporting elegant formals and tuxes, the eight seniors were seated on plush benches in the extended bed of the truck under a royal-purple vaulted satin-and-canvas tarp painted with stars and held up with exposed two-by-four beams. For the ceremonial unloading, the hydraulic end-gate was lowered to the ground with each couple on it. All who saw it and photographed it agreed that it was the last word in elegance and that the kids had looked so grown up when they stepped off the end gate and sashayed through the double doors into the gym.

*   *   *   *   *   *   *   *   *   *

25

ON THIS DAY IN 1988 WITH ETHEL OFF SUBSTITUTE-
teaching and his daughter in school, Harold Mire set a new personal
record for cleaning the farmhouse: ninety-three minutes and forty-
two seconds with no stops. "Cleaning" was what they called it, and
he did pull the vacuum cleaner around the house at breakneck
speed and slosh out the toilet bowl, of course, but his main duty
was not cleaning exactly—it was more like a redistribution of the
contents of the house to create new stacks of the paper boxes and
magazines that formed the decorating scheme in the Mire house.
His last cleaning job was to reload the closets and put the safety
on.

* * * * * * * * * * *

26

ON THIS SPRING DAY IN 1982 HAROLD MIRE LOOKED
out the west window of the house into the yard and saw two cot-
tontail rabbits in a courtship ritual. What else could it be? They
would sit in the dandelions and grass facing each other and then
all of a sudden they would leap into the air, straight up, drop
gracefully, and streak around the yard at maximum velocity before
coming back for more jumping. Harold had Ethel take a look.

Harold said, "It would save a lot of time and trouble and money
if human beings would jump up and down on a lawn instead of
going to concerts and selecting china patterns."

Ethel said, "Concerts? China patterns? What country do they
do that in?"

* * * * * * * * * * *

27

THE TEMPERATURE WAS ALREADY EIGHTY DEGREES
by midmorning today in 1988 and the sun was bright, so Ethel
Mire decided to go ahead and hang up a load of wash on the outside

line in spite of the high wind from the south that was lifting shingles on the workshop roof. The cats were hiding inside the chicken shed with disgusted expressions on their faces.

The clothes were desert-bone dry in twelve minutes, if the single towel that had not been blown off the line was any indication. It took most of the day for Harold and Ethel to retrieve the last of the clothes by driving and scouring with binoculars the four or five sections of land north of their place.

Three of Harold's army-surplus socks were never found. Harold thought Ethel's flowered blouse she had been wearing since high school was now thankfully gone for good, too, but on May 29 Porky, the neighbor's dog, brought it into the yard in one piece.

On May 30 Harold saw a half-page photo on the front page of the *Banner* featuring a pair of Penney's brief-style shorts impaled on the Boxelder city antenna on top of the grain elevator. The editor said the owner could claim them at the office if he would provide the identifying characteristics.

*   *   *   *   *   *   *   *   *   *

28
MINNESOTA BIGFOOT WAS SIGHTED AND STOPPED by the Highway Patrol today in 1988 for not wearing his seatbelt, but the officer elected not to ticket him and make him pay the $10 fine in view of the fact that the front seats had been removed and Bigfoot was driving from the back seat to get adequate legroom.

*   *   *   *   *   *   *   *   *   *

29
WHEN MORTWOOD LUMBER CAME IN WITH THE LOW bid for building Ron and Marna Vebern's new house today in 1987, it included two special items as part of the price:

1. Bleachers were to be constructed under the ash trees for his friends and neighbors, several of whom had already purchased season tickets. Daily admission would be a dollar. Free parking would be available on the diverted acres east

of the barn. Guided tours would be on demand for an extra charge.

2. Plywood concession stand. Ron's two boys would be offering soft drinks, tap beer, brats and burgers, pizza slices, snow cones, and souvenirs.

Ron was himself installing a suggestion box at the entrance gate. Unsigned suggestions would not be read. Marna would be in charge of the video sales of "Our New House" and would also be executive producer of it.

*   *   *   *   *   *   *   *   *   *

30

ON THIS MEMORIAL DAY IN 1988 HAROLD SAID TO Ethel, "Well, we might as well risk our lives on the road and go visit the cemetery."

Ethel said, "Just once I wish I could go someplace with you on a holiday and not have to be subjected to the 'Bozos on the Road' speech."

"It's the truth. It's the worst day of the year. You know it."

"Yes, I know it. Are we going?"

"Okay, but if we don't make it, don't say I didn't tell you so."

Harold and Ethel made it to the Pine Creek Cemetery, east of Fremson, and had a good time during the day, eating a little lunch and talking to their old friends and relatives who were still above ground and decorating the graves of the people they loved who weren't: uncles, aunts, cousins, nephews, fathers, mothers.

On the way home in the dark, a bozo tail-gated Harold without dimming his lights and then passed at an intersection. Harold said, "This is the last time I'm going anyplace on Memorial Day."

"I wish you wouldn't talk like that," Ethel said. "One of these days it could be true."

*   *   *   *   *   *   *   *   *   *

31

ON THIS NIGHT IN 1988 AT A FUND-RAISER PARTY for Hubert ("Skip") Humphrey III, Minnesota Bigfoot was sighted eating iced shrimp and sauce at the buffet table. He left without giving a donation as requested, but he did shake Skip's hand and say what sounded like "Hey." Skip said they needed more people like Bigfoot in the Democrat-Farmer-Labor camp. Bigfoot thought they already had enough.

*   *   *   *   *   *   *   *   *   *

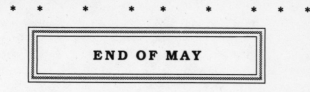

END OF MAY

JUNE

1 ED SHUBLER'S PASSIVE-SOLAR PYRAMID OF THE Living opens every year on this day in Dindan, Minnesota, and remains open until Ed is sick of visitors, which is almost immediately. Ed designed the pyramid to be his home, where he would be surrounded by his earthly possessions before he died, not after. It is a mountain of collected field-rocks with a winding tunnel that connects to a central room with a bath. The idea was that the rocks would heat up in the spring and summer and the stored heat could be used all winter. And then by the time the weather outside warmed up, the rocks would be cold again and Ed's pyramid would be cool. But the fact is that the Passive-Solar Pyramid of the Living has always been a living hell in the summer and an icebox in the winter. In 1988 Ed was still living with his earthly possessions in a camper van near the south slope of his pyramid.

* * * * * * * * * *

2 HIGH SCHOOL REUNION SEASON BEGINS. IF YOU'VE been out of school for more than twenty years and do not want Chicken Kiev stuffed in your ear, be careful about using the phrase "well preserved" to compliment the woman next to you that you assume is your old social-science teacher but who in reality was the Prom Queen the year you graduated.

* * * * * * * * * *

3 THE FAMILY REUNION SEASON IS GATHERING momentum now. You don't have to go to the family reunion this year—nobody's forcing you—but it wouldn't hurt you to make an effort to go this year, would it? When was the last time you went? Can you even remember? Just once I wish all you brothers and sisters could get there. Is it a big strain to make some baked beans and drive down for the day? How bad could it be?

* * * * * * * * * *

4 ON THIS DAY IN 1984 DENNY NELSON WAS SLIGHTLY peeved about low grain prices and government programs that required him to devote too much time in his agricultural week to filling out papers for people who earned more than he did and knew less about what went on the bottom line. That was his opinion. He was tempted to sell his machinery and all but eighty acres and buy a team of oxen and a wooden plow. His wife said she wished he would come up with a solution that was less radical. So he did.

One year later on this day, Denny opened his Aerobic Exercise Farm, for people who had got their fill and then some with hopping up and down in their living room or dancing in front of a mirror or going to a gym where young, tanned people pranced around in tight clothing. He was pleasantly surprised to find that flabby customers from Minnesota's urban centers were willing to pay up to $500 a week for cardiovascular hay baling, manure spreading, soybean weeding, and corn scooping.

Denny had always said you couldn't pay him enough to paint a house or shingle it, and here he was with clients who were paying him for the privilege of doing it themselves.

Denny Nelson's Aerobic Farm has been booked solid from March through November since his grand opening, and his income from people getting thin and healthy the natural way was such that he now can support his habit of farming. "It gets in a guy's blood," he says.

*   *   *   *   *   *   *   *   *

5 EVERY YEAR ON THIS DAY OR VERY CLOSE TO IT JOE Johnson digs out the big Rand McNally road atlas and his reading glasses and studies all the state maps. Look at those roads. So many roads. This year we're gonna get in the car and just drive and stop where we want to. Maybe take a spin up toward the Canadian border and let the spirit grab us. Or try the Painted Desert.

"What do you say?" he says to Rosemary. This is what she

says: "Joe, honey, anyplace you want to go is fine with me. You know how I like to travel."

But when the two weeks they have scheduled for vacation come, they pack the car and head north on Minnesota 12 toward the lake. Joe could drive it with his eyes closed, which is one of Rosemary's fears. Pretty soon they turn on the road by the bait shop and end up at the Pine Bough Hideaway, where they get Cabin 3, which Miles Anderson would no sooner rent to somebody else during this two-week period than he would put carpeting in his cabins, the way they do across the lake. "How many years you been comin' up here, Joe?"

In 1988 Joe said, "It's been thirty-five years, Miles. Thirty-five years."

And they go inside Cabin 3 and put their clothes in the drawers and their food in the refrigerator and Joe says, "Boy, this is the life."

Rosemary says, "What do you want for supper?"

"Tell you what—I'm going out and catch myself some bluegills. I'll be back in an hour. Miles's got the boat all ready. You want to go along?" She did and she didn't. But she always did.

*   *   *   *   *   *   *   *   *   *

6 TORNADO SEASON IS IN FULL SWING TODAY. IF YOU find yourself outside in a storm with a suitcase in your hand and a ticket in your pocket and you think the train you hear coming from the southwest will take you to Minneapolis, you could be right.

*   *   *   *   *   *   *   *   *   *

7 DARLENE AND GROVER TOBY FINALLY BIT THE bullet on this day in 1983 and decided to get rid of the green chair they bought at a funeral-home auction they don't know when. It was known as "his chair" but they were both sick of it. It had been sitting in the same spot in their living room for so long that the

Mediterranean-style legs had made holes through the linoleum and indentations in the wavy pine flooring. The chair's permanent position had always been under the hole in the ceiling that was partly patched with Scotch tape and newspaper. On windy days eighty-year-old dust would sprinkle the chair's occupant, and sometimes even a desiccated mouse-turd would come tumbling down and bounce off Grover's head.

Hanging directly behind and above the chair, on the east wall, was *Storm Clouds Gather o'er the Plains of Yesteryear*, an oil painting produced by Darlene's Aunt Lydia during her weather phase. The left front leg of the green chair, as you sit in it, was eroded and loose because of the repeated abuse from Grover's hitting it with his foot almost every night when he journeyed to the bathroom in the dark. His big toe was also a sight to behold: green and yellow, with a toenail that had been loosened by the same abuse.

Grover carried the green chair out to the red barn and stored it next to the old stove, just in case. A guy never knew. He took *Storm Clouds* out there as well, but Darlene made him bring it back.

*   *   *   *   *   *   *   *   *   *

8

ON THIS DAY IN 1952 HUD BEAMER INVENTED WHAT he called the "continuous-clean oven." Your oven-cleaning days are over, he told people. "That oven will stay spic and span just from day-to-day baking." The critics said there was no way on earth you could get the American public to buy a continuous-clean oven that everything stuck to and burnt onto eventually anyway and then you couldn't scrape it off because that would ruin the surface that kept it continuously clean. Hud drifted into obscurity and had no patent pending.

The critics were right until 1972, when all of a sudden people couldn't get in line quick enough to buy a continuous-clean oven, even though about all you could do with it when it got crusted and scaly was trade it in on a new oven that would be continuously clean until it got dirty.

*   *   *   *   *   *   *   *   *   *

9

AT THE BEGINNING OF THIS DAY IN 1988 MOST OF Minnesota's 962 stand-up comedians were still asleep and the 137 comedy clubs in the Twin Cities were empty. By late afternoon the Comedy War had broken out, after Minneapolis Local No. 12 of the United Stand-ups attacked the Laughing Biffy, a scab club in St. Paul. By midnight only three comedy clubs had survived and only eight card-carrying comedians had a sense of humor left.

* * * * * * * * * *

10

ON THIS DAY IN 1985 GOPHER STATE ENTREPRENEUR Bob Humde (inventor of the CowPie Key Hider and the Composto-Carb) tested his Whole House Vacuum Cleaner after days, even weeks, of development. He anchored the diesel-powered suction device on the lawn of his brother-in-law's house and ran the twenty-four-inch reinforced conduit to the rubber bonnet attached to the frame of the open front door. He opened all the windows in the rear of the house and brought the diesel up to speed.

Bob's vacuum cleaner removed hair from the carpets, dirt from sofa cushions, bugs from under the sink, lint off of sweaters, and all in a matter of seconds. It also removed sweaters off of hangers, paintings from the walls, drapes right off the rods, pots and pans, and the contents of the library, including his sister's Great Books of the Western World. By the time Bob got the Whole House Vacuum Cleaner shut down, his sister's three Persian cats had skidded and clawed all the way from the laundry room to the entryway. Another fraction of a second and diplomatic relations with his sister would have been severed completely instead of fractured. Bob dismantled his bright idea and put the diesel engine back on the irrigation pump where he got it.

* * * * * * * * * *

11

A TORNADO TOUCHED DOWN ON THIS DAY IN 1984 and scored a direct hit on the Pierson place. From his porch a mile away across the bean field, the Piersons' nearest neighbor, Art Hanson, said he went to the cellar right after he saw the Pierson place disintegrate and rise into the air in tiny pieces. But when he came back up, there was his neighbors' place looking the way it had three hours before, with the sun shining on it and a couple of buildings that needed paint.

Art said it was the darnedest thing, and so did Norm Pierson, who had crawled out of his cellar hoping that at least the granary had survived: that meant his family would have a place to live while they rebuilt everything. But nothing needed rebuilding; it was all there: the barns, the cattle in the yard, the sheep, the cats, even the rain gauge on the pole by the pumphouse, which showed that almost an inch had fallen in thirty minutes. Upset by the excitement, Norm went to the bathroom medicine cabinet and reached for his Alka-Seltzer, but it was gone.

"That was the only thing we ever missed," he told the newspaper. "The Pepto-Bismol was there, so I took a couple of tablespoons of that." Norm was funny, no getting around that.

In a way it was humorous, but in many other ways it was not: what the Piersons did not know was that the tornado had put them in a situation comedy set in Minnesota called "Look What the Wind Blew In." Everything the Piersons did now was accompanied by a laugh track, and after something big happened—Norm tearing his shirt off his back—there was a break for commercials. But they didn't know this, either, and had no way of finding out.

*   *   *   *   *   *   *   *   *   *

12

ON THIS DAY IN 1985 BIRD DOG BRAND TURKEY wieners were given a Turkey Oscar at the Owatonna Turkey Awards Festival. Bird Dog Brand Turkey Wieners were judged to be cheaper than the other kind and just as good in their own way.

Bird Dogs had also logged the lowest incidence of squirting and accidental launching from charcoal grills.

* * * * * * * * * *

13

ON THIS WARM NIGHT IN 1984 WITH THE POLLEN count high and his bedroom window wide open, Ivan Crump whistled and snorted in his sleep next to his wife. He first offered his rendition of "The Wabash Cannonball" through his nose, providing percussion with his vibrating lips on the exhale portion of the snore cycle. Then Ivan shifted abruptly to Bach's Toccata and Fugue in D and was five bars into it when his wife gave him a big thump with her butt and put an end to the concert.

If it had been "Your Cheatin' Heart" she might have waited. It was her favorite song, because she had seen Hank Williams once at a radio station and he had winked at her on his way out to his car. He was something. But so was Ivan, in a different sort of way.

14

This Minnesota day is sponsored by the publishers of **COMMUNICATING WITH THE GUYS WHO FIX YOUR HOUSE,** helpful dramatizations of real-life situations for the homeowner who wishes to increase the chances of early release from repair bondage to plumbers, electricians, carpenters, painters, roofers, and all the rest.

The following is a small excerpt from the carpentry section of the chapter called "Getting Them Out There," reprinted by permission of the author, "Mr. X," whose name has been changed and whose family has been relocated to a different state as part of the Federal Homeowner Protection program.

HOMEOWNER: Sorry to call you so early, but a big hole developed in my roof over the kitchen and I got birds flying in and dew dripping on my Wheaties.

[Mr. X: A light approach sometimes works. Weeping never does.]

CARPENTER: That's not the roof I put on, is it?

[MR. X: Chances are it is, but that doesn't mean there's a connection, so play that down and avoid laying guilt on him.]

HOMEOWNER: Yeah, it is, but it's not your fault. I think the lumber broke or something.

CARPENTER: I'll be right out.

[MR. X: "I'll be right out" means somewhere between three days and a week, if you're lucky. But it was a mistake in the first place to use the phone. A repair disaster is not taken seriously unless you drive to the shop and discuss it face-to-face with the repair person. Don't shave or shower.]

☞TALKING AT THE SHOP

CARPENTER: What's that white dust you got all over your head?

HOMEOWNER: That's what I would like to know. It was in the ceiling that collapsed. The kitchen is now open to the ravages of nature.

[MR. X: Avoid cute or flowery language.]

CARPENTER: When do you need it done?

[MR. X: The biggest question in the trades and the most loaded.]

HOMEOWNER: Whenever you can get to it. No big rush.

[MR. X: Never say "No big rush" to be polite. This can extend the waiting period to several months or even a decade. "Whenever you can get to it" is pure folly.]

CARPENTER: How does Friday sound?

[MR. X: Ask him which Friday. If he says this *Friday, that means Monday at the earliest.]*

CARPENTER: I can't get to it this week.

[MR. X: That means he can't get to it next week either.]

CARPENTER: I can't get to it today.

[MR. X: That means he can't get to it tomorrow either.]

HOMEOWNER: Could you just come out and look at it?

CARPENTER: Looking won't do any harm. I'll swing by this afternoon.

  [MR. X: Don't bet on it.]

CARPENTER: It might be in the morning, though. I've got two jobs ahead of you. You're on the list.

  [MR. X: Ask what list: see Appendix A for discussion of lists you can get on and what determines your position. The waste-matter list is a bad one, and the top of it is the worst position. But no matter what list it is, you'd better go ahead and cover the hole with a tarp and anchor it down with bricks.]

*   *   *   *   *   *   *   *   *

15

ON THIS DAY IN 1986 MINNESOTA BIGFOOT'S BIG hairy feet were sighted sticking out from under his black robe as he marched into the gymnasium with the faculty at Prairie Gate College and took a folding chair in the front row. The commencement address was entitled "The Past and the Future." The speaker was very proficient at bold gestures and emphatic leaning over the lectern, but Bigfoot lost the conceptual thread early in the preamble.

The man next to him was wearing a hood that indicated he had a doctorate and suede shoes made of pork skin that indicated he was from the English Department. The woman on his left was wearing perfume that made Bigfoot's eyes water and his ears ring.

As the speaker put everything he had into inflating himself for the grand challenge to the graduates, in which he would pass the symbolic torch of learning, Bigfoot drifted from a mild glassy-eyed stupor into full unconsciousness and pitched forward. Four members of the janitorial staff entered in a crouch, discreetly wrestled Bigfoot onto a handcart, and pushed him outside, where he came to his senses.

*   *   *   *   *   *   *   *   *

16

ON THIS DAY IN 1988 HAROLD MIRE DECIDED TO drive all the way to the county seat and give the new Gopher Supermarket the once-over. The grand opening had been two weeks before, but Harold wouldn't have gone near the place then for a bag of free potato chips and a quarter-pounder hot dog if his life depended on it. Life was too short as it was. Today he only got as far as the parking lot. He didn't even kill the engine. Fear gripped his heart. He was sure those smiling people flocking toward the huge automatic doors would never come out again. It was a horrible trick with loss-leader mayonnaise and tomato sauce as bait. It was grocery hell. Wide are the gates. Maybe he'd feel better tomorrow.

*   *   *   *   *   *   *   *   *   *

17

HAROLD MIRE BIT BACK HIS FEAR TODAY IN 1988 and made it through the automatic doors of the Gopher Super-market. The new cart he grabbed already had one wheel that would do nothing but skid and another wheel that fluttered so bad, Harold was not able to move down the aisles in a straight line unless he pointed the nose of the cart toward the shelves and walked side-ways. Every ten steps or so, in order to maintain control of his shopping vehicle, he had to make a complete circle around it. He abandoned the enfeebled cart near a tower of canned tuna and went home.

*   *   *   *   *   *   *   *   *   *

18

HAROLD WAS DETERMINED TO BUY SOMETHING AT the Gopher Supermarket today. It had become personal. If he didn't do it he would be haunted by failure. In the doors, smooth cart, courage up, but at the end of every aisle there was a woman wearing a surgical mask and gloves. They had such sad looks on their faces that Harold couldn't say no. He ate gooey stuff on crackers and things stuck on toothpicks and shot down mystery liquids from little plastic cups.

At home, Ethel asked him what he got. "Indigestion," he said. "I burped so much on the way back my ears were popping from the pressure built up inside the car."

"What's that stuck on your cheek?" she said.

"Well, if it has a pimiento in it, it's the turkey-and-cottage-cheese-olive dip. They had it plastered on a four-ply radial Lebanese tortilla chip."

*   *   *   *   *   *   *   *   *   *

19 IT WAS DO OR DIE ON THIS DAY IN 1988. HAROLD Mire wore dark glasses and marched into the Gopher Supermarket without selecting a cart and marched straight to paper towels and bought three rolls for a dollar and marched to Checkout Lane No. 45 down near Patagonia if the Gopher Supermarket was South America.

The assistant manager threw a lei around Harold's neck and kissed him on both cheeks, and then helped Harold place the towels on the moving belt that led to the cash register. Harold and the assistant manager and the checkout girl were all amazed by how nice a day it was. This was weather they agreed. And they were saying it was gonna be even nicer tomorrow. Harold said that's what he heard.

Fifty yards down the belt a guy was bagging his towels, one roll per sack. "Need some help with these today?"

"No, I think I can handle it," Harold said.

*   *   *   *   *   *   *   *   *   *

20 HAROLD MIRE SPENT THIS DAY IN 1988 DECOMpressing from his close encounters with the Gopher Supermarket. He sorted nuts and bolts in the workshop, tore new grease rags from the old bedsheets, and put the tools away that were strung all over the bench and floor. He also spent some quality time staring out the fly-specked windows at nothing in particular.

*   *   *   *   *   *   *   *   *   *

21 MINNESOTA BIGFOOT WAS SIGHTED TODAY IN 1987 paying full sticker price *plus* dealer prep, delivery, and license on a new car. The salesman flapped his sports jacket and crowed to his colleagues until the down-payment check bounced. Bigfoot had selected loons for his decorative outdoor checks, but had deposited only $5 in his new account.

*   *   *   *   *   *   *   *   *   *

22 HAROLD MIRE SMELLED PINE SMOKE TODAY IN 1988 before he saw it. When he told his daughter, Lily, about it, they decided to find the fire. They had always liked going to natural disasters together. They drove for an hour toward the source of the smoke and were almost there, but Lily had a meeting with the youth group at church, so they drove back home. That night on the evening news Harold found out that the smoke was from a Canadian forest fire five hundred miles away. He guessed they had imagined seeing the flames then, but Harold was proud of his nose nevertheless. It was a new distance record for him, breaking the old record, when he had smelled perfume in the yard and followed the scent to Mortwood, four miles away. The Avon lady had dropped a vial of toilet water from her shipment on the sidewalk outside the post office. Good as his nose was, though, Harold would be the first to say that it had its drawbacks when it came to a closed room with too many nervous people in it.

*   *   *   *   *   *   *   *   *   *

23

MINNESOTA BIGFOOT WAS SIGHTED AT A GROOM'S
Dinner in the Twin Cities suburb of Golden Vale this day in 1985.
Bigfoot laughed like crazy and knocked his beer bottle over when
a couple of guys brought out a huge inflated plastic object in a
shape common to the male of their species. Boy, this was a hooter!!
Bigfoot wouldn't miss the wedding tomorrow for anything—it had
to be a riot. Maybe he could live with these people after all—they
were more primitive than he had originally thought.

* * * * * * * * * *

24

ON THIS DAY IN 1985 MINNESOTA BIGFOOT WAS
sighted at the Methodist church in Golden Vale sitting by himself
in the choir loft. The music was pretty good, he thought, but he
kept waiting for more inflated objects to be paraded before the
crowd, to lighten up the ceremony. But not one funny thing happened. Some people were crying. He was baffled. Except for the
kiss afterward and the absence of the coffin, it was a lot like
the funeral he had attended. The groom looked like he might
have been right at home in a grave, but he stood under his own
power.

After the photos, Bigfoot was sighted in the basement having
a little lunch and wedding cake while the bride and groom took
the wrappers off lamps and mixers and bowls and towels. That was
funnier.

Things picked up when the bride and groom came out the door
of the church and people threw rice on them and then they saw
their car and were bowled over: it was all covered with shaving
cream and tin cans hanging from the bumper. This was getting
good. And then some boys chased behind the bride and groom in
their cars with no tin cans but with the horns honking like mad. It
was worth waiting for. This was the kind of low comedy Bigfoot
had grown up with; he laughed so much his stomach hurt.

* * * * * * * * * *

25

ON THIS EVENING IN 1986 HAROLD MIRE WAS drinking iced tea and sitting on the elm-stump chair he had carved with a chain saw. When he heard the distant whistle of the Burlington Northern freight headed south toward Sioux Falls, he remembered the train ride he had taken with his family to Kansas City to visit an aunt who collected tiny bear statues and an uncle who collected dust. That made him think of his pal Eddie, who brought a fruit jar of his fingernail clippings to seventh-grade science.

The freight whistled again and Harold saw himself standing in the yard of the Fremson Farmer's Elevator in 1956, surrounded by his fellow Fremson High School seniors. They all turned at once when they heard the whistle of the passenger train at the crossing where the year before Mitch Drees had pretended to run out of gas in his Buick. The through freight had hit it on schedule and carried it three hundred yards to the quarry, where it became a permanent source of fascination to grade-school kids on field trips. Mitch's big plan was to take the insurance money and go to California. It was dumb to put his car on the tracks, and dumber not to pay the premium on the car insurance first, but that's what kept him out of jail.

Thirty-one years later, in 1987, on a long-overdue family vacation, Harold would see Mitch at the San Diego Zoo, near the elephant ride. He would be wearing a name tag and his job would be to guide the elephant around the track and make it stop so the happy children on its back could have their picture taken by happy parents. But in 1986, sipping iced tea on a stump, Harold didn't know he would see Mitch again. He also didn't know that his daughter would ride the camel instead of the elephant. In fact, he didn't know anything about the future at that point: his or anybody else's. He guessed he would get up and go inside pretty soon.

*   *   *   *   *   *   *   *   *

26

IT WAS THE NEXT WARM EVENING IN JUNE OF 1986 when Harold was on the elm-stump chair with more iced tea when he remembered that the freight whistle last night had made him remember his senior trip to Chicago thirty years ago, but Mitch Drees had stepped in with his mangled Buick.

The nine seniors had been standing by the grain elevator's coal shed because Mr. Handeen, the Fremson Consolidated superintendent and chaperon, had arranged for the passenger train to make a special stop for this second-to-last graduating class ever and the last to take a senior trip.

Harold's class shot the works on Chicago, and a little more besides. He wished he could remember more about it, since it was historic. But it came down to three items:

1. Descending into the realistic coal mine at the Chicago Museum of Science and Industry and listening to the simulated miner who illustrated the drilling machinery in a loud voice nobody could understand.
2. Talking to three girls from his class who were wearing only pajamas in their room at the Drake Hotel.
3. Tripping while running across the street in front of the hotel and tearing both knees out of his black gabardine suit pants and soaking up a pool of oil with the back of his white shirt as he lay there trying to figure out how he would get back in through the lobby and past the bellhop. It was no more than he deserved, though, for having lusted in his heart the night before and kissing one of the girls on the neck.

*   *   *   *   *   *   *   *   *   *

27

BECAUSE THE STRAP WAS BITING INTO HER shoulder today in 1987 and the main zipper compartment was developing stress lines, Dorothy Stender, of rural Big Stone County, dumped the contents of her purse on the dining-room table (after putting in all the extra leaves), and separated the items into throw-away and keep. The keep pile was further divided into keep-in-purse and keep-someplace-else.

The keep-someplace-else pile was divided into fifteen designated-area piles:

1. Little drawer on left top of dresser.
2. Green plastic bag in back of bathroom closet.
3. Plaid box under Christmas decorations on top shelf of pantry.
4. Vegetable drawer of refrigerator.
5. Gray barrel in chicken shed.
6. Trunk of car.
7. Oven.
8. Plastic jewelry-tray on back of toilet.
9. Sleeve of good coat.
10. Pocket of parka.
11. Old mint container from Oshkosh.
12. Porch ledge.
13. Clothes hamper.
14. Button box.
15. Big Stone Library.

On this same day in 1987 Maureen Parkett of New Riviera, Minnesota, used a different method to organize her purse. She removed her billfold and car keys and threw everything else in the trash burner, including the purse. She was starting a new life without that bum she met at Mammoth Cave two years ago. "Good riddance" were the operative words today. She was clearing the decks.

*   *   *   *   *   *   *   *   *   *

28

ON THIS NIGHT IN 1985 BIGFOOT WAS SIGHTED IN a crowd of revelers engaging in a chivaree on the lawn in front of 1344 Bingle Lane in Golden Vale, where quite by accident he had been shuffling by and recognized guests from the Methodist wedding a week ago. He had no idea what was happening but it looked promising. He overheard a man telling how he had sneaked in the house and short-sheeted the bed and put sand in something. Everybody was banging on pots with spoons and yelling at the house.

Pretty soon the front door opened and what a surprise!! It was the bride and groom and they weren't mad at all; they invited everybody in for barbecues, and bars, and potato chips, and coffee, which by pure luck they had plenty of ready.

*   *   *   *   *   *   *   *   *   *

29 HAROLD MIRE HAD FINALLY AGREED WITH ETHEL
in early 1988 that he did have a high-frequency hearing loss, and
it was probably caused by the chain saw, the air-compressor pump,
the lawn mower, the rototiller, and a bunch of other noisy machinery, beginning with the bun extruder in the bakery years ago.

Then last month, during his brother Bill's visit, Harold heard
Bill say he was going to send his dog to college.

"That mutt?" Harold said.

Ethel interpreted, as she had begun to do: "He said his daughter
was going to Colorado, Harold." Harold usually got the consonants
right anyway.

But today in 1988 something new developed: Harold was at
the cafe for the first time in weeks and at one point in the free-for-
all conversation he said, "You must've brought the corn along."

And Blaine said, "What's this about a muslin-wrapped arm?"

And Don said, "Did you sprain it? You do seem to favor it."

Harold repeated what he had said, but he didn't say what
he thought: now, evidently, he had a high-frequency *speaking*
loss, too.

Back home, Harold told Ethel she'd better think about trading
him in. She had him name the men at the table and then she said,
"They're all farmers and all about your age. Chances are they have
high-frequency hearing losses, too. That's what noisy tractors will
do. And like you, Harold, they probably won't wear ear protectors
around loud machinery to keep it from getting worse."

"It's a lot of trouble, they get in the way," Harold said.

"What? You're eating truffles to lose weight?"

"I said, 'Okay, okay, I'll make an effort to wear the protectors.'"

*   *   *   *   *   *   *   *   *   *

30 MINNESOTA BIGFOOT WAS SIGHTED WALKING
across the border into South Dakota on this day in 1987 to buy
firecrackers at Jim Boom's All-American Fireworks. He came out
with a sack of bottle rockets, lady fingers, sparklers, and bangballs.

Then, in direct violation of the law, Bigfoot walked back into Minnesota and shot off the whole arsenal, but he didn't have any fun at all and singed the hair on his arm with a sparkler besides. Everybody was doing it, so he had thought he'd try it—but it was like drinking diet pop or bowling, he couldn't understand what pleasure these people derived from it. He had a lot to learn about the entertainment value of explosives he guessed.

* * * * * * * * * *

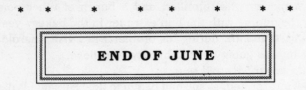

END OF JUNE

JULY

1 YOU COULD MOVE INTO YOUR HOUSE TODAY THAT you bought last month and be so happy that the deal went through and the interest rates were not too bad and the owners came down a little on the asking price but nobody got hurt on it and it is such a peaceful neighborhood, and you could open the garage door to drive the car in and notice this big pipe sticking up in the center of the floor that would tear the oil pan off and who knows what else, and the pipe could lead to an underground tank half full of something that smells like gasoline only worse, and the previous owners, the Smiths, through their lawyer could tell you that they were sure they mentioned that they had always let their neighbors on the north, in the house with the painted-black windows, use the garage to work on their dune buggies and Harleys and to fuel up from the underground tank before they went out on a ride, all part of a bartering arrangement whereby the nuclear family of bikers would try not to rev up their bigger machines after midnight in exchange for the Smith family's not calling the police when the bikers slept on the Smiths' lawn in their birthday suits, and the Smiths could be sure you might have the same amicable arrangement.

* * * * * * * * * *

2 MINNESOTA BIGFOOT WAS SIGHTED COMING OUT OF the grove of trees and joining the mob at the starting line of a five-mile fun run in Mortwood on this day in 1987. He had no idea what was going on, but he kept moving anyway after the gun went off. At the two-mile mark, Bigfoot was overtaken by two visiting ministers from the Twin Cities who tried to convert him to Lutheranism, whatever that was. At the four-mile mark, Bigfoot ducked back into the trees and sat down. Just when he thought he was beginning to understand these people, something like this had to happen.

* * * * * * * * * *

3 THE QUESTION TODAY THIS YEAR, IS: *SHOULD YOU build an addition on your house?* Right now your house is small enough so that when you are in the shower and forget to get a towel out of the closet, you can yell above the sound of the water and your wife or husband or the kids can hear you and get one for you. But if you erect that fifteen-hundred-square-foot family room on the west there and they are in it watching videos, you could yell till you were blue in the face and end up slipping and sliding over to the towels yourself anyway. This could lead to a total breakdown in family communication. Before you know it, that beautiful addition where you had meant to gather and play checkers and read out loud to each other could be up for sale with the house.

*   *   *   *   *   *   *   *   *   *

4 A GUY CAN TALK UNTIL HE'S BLUE IN THE FACE ON the Fourth of July and tell you to stay off the roads, off the beaches, and out of the parks and swimming pools on this day, but do you think he doesn't know you won't listen?

*   *   *   *   *   *   *   *   *

5 This day brought to you by the BEAUTIFUL HERITAGE SOCKET SET, finely crafted socket wrenches in a walnut-grained plywood presentation case that speaks quality. The price is an incredible $99.95. Please specify whether you wish the standard or metric socket set. Your family will cherish it for years. From BEAUTIFUL HERITAGE, mass producers of limited-edition collectibles since 1981.

*   *   *   *   *   *   *   *   *   *

6

THE PEAT MOSS PAGEANT IS HELD TODAY IN Bogworth, Minnesota, honorary hometown of Mr. Rick Borg, the founder of the Minnesota Pageant Council, current peat-moss liaison officer at the State Capitol, and the man responsible for introducing peat-moss dishes into the Minnesota school-lunch program. This festive day begins with the 10K Peat Moss Slog across the spongy terrain west of town and ends at the football field with a huge peat-moss-and-pork feed.

* * * * * * * * * *

7

Another day brought to you by BIGGER HAMMER HARDWARE and another story from their files. The facts are true—the name has been changed to Harvey.

☞HANDYMAN HARVEY'S STORY

My plan was to save a few bucks and do my own electrical wiring in the remodeled kitchen. I guess I really didn't completely understand the difference between 220 volts and 110. I had a book on it, but some pages were torn out. It was unclear to me what that third bare wire was for. I was home free, I thought in my pride. The toaster toasted like mad but then it melted into the new Formica countertop and just after I got the fire out the refrigerator made a sound like a car with all four brakes locked and then stopped. When I turned on the portable fan to clear some of the smoke, it took off and flew through my new triple-pane window.

I'm not saying it was the biggest mistake of my handyman career. The time I put the shingles upside down on the garage was a doozy, and right out there where everybody could see it. I got in the paper on that one. This time I had BIGGER HAMMER to lean on. They were at my place for two days and didn't make one smart remark or act like know-it-alls even though they are.

* * * * * * * * * *

8

ON THIS DAY IN 1987 DONALD R. OLSEN WALKED through the midway at the Yellow Medicine County Fair and was so swept up by the excitement that he stopped to dine standing up at one of the food trailers. Two hours later, lying down, Mr. Olsen had attached an addendum to his philosophy: You only go around once, but if you eat a bad corn dog, halfway around is about the most you can expect or even want.

*   *   *   *   *   *   *   *   *   *

9

THE ENDLESS PARADE WAS KICKED OFF IN GAROSE, Minnesota, on this day in 1985 after a speech by the mayor. All 230 units of the parade went by the reviewing stand. And then here they came again, and again, and again, led by the high-school band in wool uniforms, and the Cub Scouts, and the Boy Scouts, and the Shriners in funny cars and hats, and the old tractors, and the queens of pork and beef and dairy in convertibles. Around and around the parade route they went, down 4th, up Willow, across the tracks and through the park, and up 3rd and down Main. Oh, the honking of the old cars, the waves from the fire trucks, the throwing of the candy to the kids!!! It was better each time they returned—they never wilted, never aged.

Pretty soon the spectators left to go about their daily business, and the sun set. But the next day more people showed up with their lawn chairs to watch the parade go by—the steam tractor, the '27 Ford, the accordion quartet, the senior citizens playing whist on a hayrack. It has never stopped. Maybe it will last forever. This perpetual parade is the closest thing to heaven we shall ever know on earth. The question is, though: how do you get your unit in the parade if it's already started and you're weary of watching?

*   *   *   *   *   *   *   *   *   *

10

IN THE AFTERNOON OF THIS DAY IN 1987 HAROLD
Mire was out wandering around in the brown grass and weeds and
bare dirt of what passed for the lawn of his acreage. He was getting
a little fresh air as he waited for a call-back from the lumberyard.
He was carrying the $12 Midnite Madness Special remote phone
he had bought against his better judgment, like some knee-jerk
consumer. It was another one of those things he didn't need but
he had it anyway. The taco rack his brother had given him for
Christmas was in the same category, except Harold had made that
into a chick feeder. The cheap phone would never rise above its
present level of incarnation.

When the phone chirped it was not Marty from the lumberyard
telling him when the treated two-by-sixes would be delivered, it
was a reporter from Gopher State Radio—Jan something—calling
from St. Paul to get Harold's opinion on the threatened hostile
takeover of Dayton's, the Minnesota darling of retail.

"Why me?" Harold said. "Did I win a contest? Or did I lose
one?"

"I picked you at random—we wanted input from Greater Minnesota."

"Greater Minnesota" had been dreamed up by the shakers at
the Capitol to replace the term "Outstate Minnesota," which they
said didn't express just how important the small towns and farms
were to those Minnesotans who lived on the cutting edge of civilization near the freeways and the Dome and the racetrack. But
Harold wasn't born yesterday: "Greater Minnesota" meant that the
heads (and the feet and fingers and noses and so on) of government
in St. Paul still thought Harold lived in a cultural desert.

But the Gopher State reporter was pleasant enough, and it was
Harold's policy to be pleasant in return—it was his Greater Minnesota charm. He talked of the thrill of riding the escalators at the
downtown Minneapolis store, and how the housewares department
made the hair on the back of his neck stand up, it was so exciting.
Basically Harold was just blathering away, the way a guy will on
the radio if he thinks it's his only chance for audio glory. Harold
was human.

Fifty feet away from Harold and his piss-ant phone, the Mire

family old mare was eating ditch hay that was too dry and dusty;
it was aggravating the horse's heaves—an asthma-like condition in
a horse, the vet had said. She was coughing to beat the band: neck
stretched out, tongue extended, the complete industrial-grade
coughing package. In the world of equine digestion—as Harold had
learned by experience—for every action there is often an equal
and opposite reaction. If the opposite reaction had not been pre-
cipitated in the present case, the mare would have moved backward
three feet with every cough. As it was she stayed roughly in one
spot, because of the balanced thrust of the two exhaust systems.

The reaction was in the baritone-bass range mostly, with some
high harmonics. The mare sounded like one-third of a polka band.
If she had been a ship in the fog, nobody would've run into her.
The duration of each event was from two to five seconds. The
recharge time was about twenty seconds. Harold could have taken
the phone to another part of the yard, or inside the house, but he
was concentrating too hard on being an articulate spokesperson.

On the Gopher State Radio Roundup that evening, Harold
listened to himself being nostalgic about Dayton's and in the background the Mire mare was adding her 2¢ to the top story of the
day. Greater Minnesota had been heard from again.

*   *   *   *   *   *   *   *   *   *

11

IN THE MIDDLE OF A DROUGHT ON THIS DAY IN 1988
with crops withering in Minnesota and all over the breadbasket of
America, Harold Mire noticed on the news that the cereal manufacturers had begun to raise their prices on puffed this and flake
that and frosted something else. The cereals were already overpriced, but the cereal producers were claiming that higher grain
prices had forced them into it. Any farmer, including the ones
suffering from the drought on this day, and including Harold's
neighbors, could tell you that the cereal manufacturers were making hay from the drought. Harold thought there ought to be a law
against that kind of behavior or at least a boycott of the long shelves
of cereals in the stores. For once Harold got complete agreement
at the cafe.

*   *   *   *   *   *   *   *   *   *

12

THE HAM FESTIVAL IS ALWAYS KICKED OFF BY A ham dinner at noon today at Sittonburg, Minnesota. Later in the day—after the ham race, and the ham-antics talent show, and the greased pig chases—a man and woman with the biggest hams and willing to appear on stage in bathing suits are crowned King and Queen of the Ham Ball and given a year's supply of stretch pants and a bowling ball. The Grand March of Hams that precedes the Ham Ball is worth the ticket price.

*   *   *   *   *   *   *   *   *   *

13

This day brought to you by OILRIG DISHWASHING LIQ-UID, for men who do their share around the house but don't want to broadcast it. Sweeping the floors, doing laundry, cooking the meals, it's not women's work, or men's work either. It's just work that has to be done no matter what your gender is. But doing dishes can be a problem for real men because most dishwashing detergents soften their hands and make them beautiful and attractive, which can be a liability at Friday-night poker. So why go to all the trouble of wearing rubber gloves at the game just so the boys can't see your lovely hands? And besides it's hard to shuffle. OILRIG used every day will keep your hands red, rough, and cracked. It's the perfect dish soap for the modern man who has to work and play around chauvinistic Neanderthals.

*   *   *   *   *   *   *   *   *   *

14

ON THIS DAY IN 1984 MINNESOTA BIGFOOT WAS sighted playing right field for Our Saviour's Lutheran at the church-league softball tournament in Roseville. Bigfoot robbed two power hitters from Holy Redeemer of home runs with his leaping one-handed catches.

*   *   *   *   *   *   *   *   *   *

15

ON THIS DAY IN 1987 MINNESOTA BIGFOOT WAS sighted at the depot in Cottonwood, Minnesota. He had been there since the day before, watching the freights go by. He was waiting for the passenger train to Minneapolis. That the last passenger train had gone through in 1962 was good news to him. That meant another one should be along any day now. It was the only way to travel.

*   *   *   *   *   *   *   *   *   *

16

THIS IS THE DAY IN 1987 WHEN ETHEL MIRE decided to throw away all clothes in her closet she hadn't worn in six years or more. What she bagged for Goodwill included the plaid circular skirt from high school she only wore to basketball games, three polyester blouses with ties at the necks and given to her on three successive Christmases by her sister-in-law, a gray wool jumper that used to go with anything but went with nothing now, and a pants suit with an elastic waistband. While she was at it she packed up Harold's twenty-year-old parka with the ripped pockets he used for a blanket when he took a nap on the living-room floor. She'd have to answer for it eventually.

*   *   *   *   *   *   *   *   *   *

17

THE FIRST PERSONAL-SIZE ELECTRONIC MOSQUITO-deterrent device worn around the waist as a belt was invented on this day in 1984. It was found to be 100 percent effective in repelling mosquitoes, but it attracted Canada geese like flies and made them madder than hornets.

*   *   *   *   *   *   *   *   *   *

18

BIGFOOT WAS SIGHTED AT THE DEMOCRATIC
National Convention in Atlanta tonight in 1988. It had been a long
trip on the bus, but he was hoping to be nominated as a favorite
upright-primate candidate by the Minnesota delegation on the first
ballot. Later, back at his hotel, Bigfoot saw a familiar face coming
toward him. It was his twin brother!! But he didn't have a twin
brother; it was only his reflection in the full-length mirror at the
end of the hall. Alone again. He was through with politics.

*   *   *   *   *   *   *   *   *

19

ON THIS DAY IN 1986 PRAIRIE MALL DIRECTOR
Douglas Donnet laughed like a dictator who had misplaced the pot
he peed in when the *Gopher Tribune* reporter asked about the
forbidden zones at the mall. What nonsense. Who have you been
talking to? Just about anybody, the reporter said. Doug was up
against the wall on this one. He had been seen on the streets with
gravy on his tie. People said he had a one-way bus ticket out of
this burg in his pocket.

Doug said to the reporter: "Swoopton is a Minnesota starship
city. We're growing both economically and culturally. The Prairie
Mall is an important piece in this puzzle of progress."

Nevertheless the mall sat at the edge of town like a giant ship
run aground on an asphalt beach. The night janitors were working
in teams now, wearing side arms and boot knives. They called
themselves the Eagle Squadron. During lunch breaks they smoked
'em if they had 'em and told stories. They remembered the night
Andy and his sack of baloney sandwiches were disassembled into
atoms in the narrow hall leading to the air-conditioner room. They
swore to it. They missed him.

*   *   *   *   *   *   *   *   *

20

ON THIS DAY IN 1986 SOME HIGH-SCHOOL KIDS dared each other to gallop into the creepy twilight at the rear of Stereo Stable and flip through the dusty album-bins. The manager was up front with his head in his hands. His last sale had been a George Jones cassette to a trucker from Montana.

* * * * * * * * * *

21

EVERYTHING IN MURPHY'S MATURE FASHIONS FOR Women was marked down way below cost on this day in 1986. It was back to bartending for Murphy. His close friends had told him long ago it was a terrible name anyway. "You can tell it's a store for larger ladies, Murph."

In '85 Murphy had upgraded to three-quarter-inch plywood after Mrs. Turkle toppled over and took out Dressing Booth No. 2. He thought heavier plywood would cure what ailed his business. But then insult had been added to injury when a woman disappeared while squeezing into a pair of slacks one size too small for her. Her husband had been out waiting in the car. He had read every scrap of paper in the glove compartment twice before he decided to check on her. It was the story of his life.

"She's in Booth Number One. See for yourself," Murphy had said. Except for the purse full of Pearson's Salted Nut Rolls, there was no trace of her. The Swoopton police said there were signs of a struggle. Murphy told them it was about par for the course.

"If this gets out, it'll ruin me," he had told the police.

"We'll try to keep a lid on it," the police had said.

* * * * * * * * * *

22

ON THIS DAY AT THE PRAIRIE MALL IN 1986 WANDA didn't sell so much as a stick of incense. She wondered what hit her, but she planned to stay at the House of Pisces gift shop until

the last dog was hung. She was about at the end of her rope. She
was beginning to see herself coming and going.

Wanda had invested her whole lump-sum divorce settlement
into the House of Pisces. It had been a dream come true until last
year, when a man from Swoopton bought a gift set of miniature
Chinese gongs for his wife's birthday. They said the husband had
then begun to float through the air of their bedroom at night, sound
asleep. They said his wife was afraid he would drift outdoors and
blow into South Dakota. Try to keep something like that quiet.

* * * * * * * * * *

23

ON THIS DAY IN 1986 MARIE OPENED THE SLIDING
doors to Towels 'n' Washcloths at nine o'clock and sat behind the
register, working crosswords and listening to the radio. She would
have turned on the overhead lights if anybody had wandered in,
but nobody did. Weeks earlier she had gone through a tough period
of self-examination and found herself blameless in this Prairie Mall
horror. But she still thought there was no justice in the universe.
Just before closing time she stood at the entrance to Towels 'n'
Washcloths and shook her finger at nobody in particular. "How
come you people don't take baths anymore!!"

* * * * * * * * * *

24

AT HARDWARE HARBOR IN THE PRAIRIE MALL, TODAY
in 1986 was no different from any other day over the last three
months: nothing worked. You bought a hammer, the head flew off.
Nails bent every which way without penetrating wood. The paint
was like glue. A customer would pick up a power drill and Hershey
would say: "It looks good, especially at that price, but the motors
have been burning out in those. If I were you I'd check at the
lumberyard."

Hershey and his partner, Hank, were playing cribbage until
closing time today, as usual, at a card table they had set up in the
aisle between plumbing and custom automotive parts. They were
a familiar fixture there. The kibitzers always showed up early,

which was a good thing for Hank, because Hershey tended to peg
more than his hand was worth.

Most people weren't afraid to go into Hardware Harbor, but
they would never have thought of buying anything. Hershey and
Hank couldn't care less. They were as mellow as they come. To
hell with hardware.

*   *   *   *   *   *   *   *   *   *

25

THIS WAS THE FIRST DAY IN A LONG TIME IN 1986
that business was almost as usual out at the Prairie Mall. A guy
from the Bureau of Land Management bought a plaid sports jacket
at Terry's Store for Men after getting Terry's attention by tapping
on the one-by-four board across the door. As long as he was in
there, he picked up a tie with a pheasant pattern and a tie clasp
shaped like a walleyed pike. The floor drains overflowed because
some elementary kids flushed all the toilets together repeatedly.
And a boy and girl sat holding hands on the bench outside the dark
entrance of Tails & Noses & Fins, oblivious to the whimpering
inside. They were in love, but the owner was in misery.

*   *   *   *   *   *   *   *   *   *

26

ON THIS DAY IN 1986 THE PRAIRIE MALL WAS
deserted. There weren't even any looters out there. Shoppers were
going back downtown. The merchants on Swoopton's main street
were giddy. But they shouldn't have counted their chickens before
they were hatched. Something was wrong at Riteway Office Equipment. The air was heavy and dark. When you entered, the clerks
turned and shuffled toward you. They didn't speak unless spoken
to. They were dressed in black.

A man named Donald came in and wanted manila folders with
tabs. They stood around him in a circle. They would check in the
basement. The others shuffled closer, touching Donald as if by
accident.

No manila folders. They could order them for him. They wanted
to know where he lived. They wanted to know if he could be

reached by phone. Donald wished he had checked for folders at the Prairie Mall first, in spite of the stories and the police barricades. He hoped it wasn't too late. But it was. The Prairie Mall was history.

* * * * * * * * * *

27

ON THIS DAY IN 1987 MINNESOTA BIGFOOT WAS sighted at the quarter-mile dirt track in Birdnose Falls, driving a modified Plymouth Fury (No. 7) for Pete's Hardware in the feature race. He won by three car lengths after the leader was black-flagged. When the track queen presented him his trophy and kissed him on the cheek, he picked her up with one hand around her waist and raised her seven feet into the air in a gesture of victory.

* * * * * * * * * *

28

TODAY ONLY, EVERY YEAR SINCE 1975 IT'S THE Gayla Annual Minnesota Emergency Poetry Liquidation Sale in the lobby of the Riverbottom Motel on Harriet Island, owned and operated by Gayla Peterson. This is the only place in Minnesota where you can pick up beautifully crafted original poems signed by the authors at below wholesale cost.

Gayla's got long poems, short poems, fat poems, thin poems, rhyming poems, and very free verse—and she's got all your favorite subjects: beef cattle, sunsets, depression, personal growth, lakes, topsoil, freeways, revolution, tall buildings, relationships, and much, much more. Gayla's prices are so low you'll want a poem for every room of your house and the garage as well. It begins at 8:00 P.M. sharp and ends at midnight. Cash only, no refunds, please bring your own containers.

* * * * * * * * * *

29

THIS DAY BEFORE THE GILFRED FAMILY REUNION in 1987 Harold and Ethel both came down with the Creeping

Crud—his sister's name for sore throat and hacking cough and general crappy feeling. Harold's mother called it the Epizoodic. Whatever it was, Harold felt like death warmed over for eighteen hours. Ethel climbed into the guest bed in the attic and stayed there all day in her nightgown.

Harold wouldn't be caught dead in pajamas even in the peak of health, but when he was sick he always remained fully dressed and propped himself up in a chair. Sometimes if he got dizzy and needed to be briefly horizontal, he would lie down on the couch but would keep one foot on the floor and not take off his shoes. He would put his head on his arm and never use a pillow. "If you ever see me in bed in the middle of the day call Primmer's." Primmer's specialized in the no-frills interment.

*   *   *   *   *   *   *   *   *   *

30
ON THIS DAY IN 1987 THE GILFRED FAMILY REUNION (Ethel's mother's side) was held as usual at the rented screened pavilion overlooking Lake Mecham, on the South Dakota border. The South Dakota Gilfreds (a vocal minority) did not like going farther than a hundred yards into Minnesota, and even then they sat at the tables on the west side, in the sun, nearest their beloved state. Harold and Ethel called in sick on this one, but they got the full report on it anyway. It was a zoo, basically, his sister-in-law said.

*   *   *   *   *   *   *   *   *   *

31
HAROLD AND ETHEL FELT MUCH BETTER TODAY IN 1987 but only until they remembered that they had three more family reunions looming on the horizon: it would be cruel and unusual picnicking. They didn't see how they could credibly stretch the Creeping Crud out that long.

Next weekend, the Mires (Harold's father's side) would be assembling at Timber Park (where they had the large shelter house reserved in perpetuity), which also happened to be the main training grounds for combat mosquitoes from five states—the still, hot, humid air was ideal for them. There was never a breeze at Timber Park, because it had been built in a natural bowl of earth, with the shelter house at the bottom. And for some reason trees wouldn't grow there, not even on the shore of the stagnant pond.

In two weeks, the Belder family reunion (Ethel's father's side) would coalesce at her Uncle Allard's big two-thousand-acre spread near Hutchinson, where the wind never stopped blowing and all the food had to be anchored to the picnic tables, except for Sally (née Belder) Mixnor's sweet-potato–sauerkraut hotdish. She brought it every year and every year it would sit there with no takers and swell up in the sun. Harold thought it actually looked more appetizing at the end of the day than it did at the beginning, not that he was ever tempted.

In three weeks, the Rudd family reunion (Harold's mother's side) would be what it always was—a full-day affair. You could come for breakfast and that way you'd get to sit around for twelve hours at City Park and watch teenagers drive by and spin their wheels and give you the finger. Two of the Rudds would sleep at the park the night before so they could be sure to get the shelter house on the hill by the flush toilets.

Harold and Ethel did make it to the last three reunions in 1987, but it left permanent scars. Things were about the same as in previous years at the reunions, but Harold's threshold was lower. Sick or not, Ethel knew when to speak and when not to, but Harold coming out of the Creeping Crud had a tendency to turn up his sarcasm, which is one of the least effective communication tools at a family reunion, right behind fistfights. And Harold's nose looked like a Beefsteak tomato from standing in the sun and pitching horseshoes three weekends in a row.

*   *   *   *   *   *   *   *   *   *

END OF JULY

AUGUST

1 THE FIRST KNOWN SIGHTING OF MINNESOTA BIGFOOT occurred on this day in 1974 at a Southdale store, where he was seen buying a pair of cotton cords with a fifty-six-inch waist and sixty-inch inseam. He also picked up a couple of short-sleeved Hawaiian shirts that were on sale. The belt he bought didn't match, but Bigfoot thought it did.

* * * * * * * * * * *

2 Today is your lucky day because you *WILL DEFINITELY WIN ONE OF THE FOLLOWING PRIZES IF YOU ACT NOW!!!!* Your name has already been selected!!!

1. Italian Villa: retail value of $7,790,000
2. One Million Dollars: retail value of $866,000
3. 400 Blond Dining-Room Suites: retail value of $400,000
4. 6 days and 5 nights at the Holiday Club campground near Lake Gumbo, west of Duluth. Does not include meals, transportation, horizontal bed, room with lockable door and windows, inoculations, or small-arms permit. Retail value: it depends.

* * * * * * * * * *

3 ON THIS DAY IN 1951 IN NEW MEXICO, THE FIRST used disposable diaper was thrown from a moving car with Minnesota plates and plastered itself on the windshield of the car behind, causing the driver to take out the whole east wall of the footprint display at Dinosaur World.

* * * * * * * * * *

4 EVERY YEAR SINCE 1982 RIGHT ABOUT NOW IN A Minnesota location traditionally announced in the personals section of *The Pioneer Press*, you have been able to attend "Cat Sailing Days." If competitive sailing of dried, flattened cats that bought the farm on blacktop roads in summer is your cup of tea, don't miss this festival. In 1988 there were three classes of competition: Beginner, Stock, and Modified (shellacking and trimming permitted). Send a SASE to the Flat Cat society and you will receive an illustrated booklet (parental guidance suggested) that explains how to recognize airfoil capabilities in a flat cat. T-shirts and mugs are also available with the familiar society logo.

* * * * * * * * * *

5 ON THIS DAY IN 1949 NORTH OF GRANITE FALLS, Minnesota, up on the ridge, a meteorite with tail fins plunged to the earth in a field: it looked exactly like a quarter-scale model baby-blue 1957 Chevy with a raked front end, although nobody knew that until eight years later, when General Motors took the wraps off its new models.

* * * * * * * * * *

6 ON THIS DAY IN 1982 BAREFOOT ACTIVIST THOMAS Peterson published *Looking Out for Number Two*, the popular chapbook that led to the passage of strict leash laws in Minneapolis.

* * * * * * * * * *

7 HOW TO USE UP THE GIANT ZUCCHINI TAKING OVER your garden by this day:

—Keep a zucchini in the car trunk to block the wheels when changing a flat tire.

—Drop a zucchini into the watermelon bin at the supermarket.

—Make a beach hat out of it.

—Dress up a big zucchini and put it in the passenger seat of your car when you commute so you can drive in the ride-share lane.

—Scare your dog by carving it into an alligator—the zucchini.

—Drill three holes in a zucchini and use it in your summer bowling league.

—Teenage girls can chain a large zucchini around their ankle to show they're going steady.

*   *   *   *   *   *   *   *   *   *

8 BIRTHDAY OF LOREN JACKSON, THE FIRST PERSON to attach a garage to his house, in 1908. Loren was a car nut and loved the smell of a hot engine and evaporating gasoline drifting through the house after he parked his car, and the clouds of blue smoke when he started it. The convenience of being able to step from his kitchen into his car was also a plus. Loren envisioned that the attached garage would become as common as suspenders. But he did not live to see the American dream come true: a chicken in every microwave and a car in all three stalls of the attached garage and some lawn furniture and paint and bicycles up in front.

*   *   *   *   *   *   *   *   *   *

9 ON THIS DAY IN 1987 JOHN PETERSON OF ALEXANDRIA suddenly decided that he was tired of mowing his half-acre of lawn with the little puker of a push mower he owned and so he went right down to Mower City and tried out one of those beautiful riding mowers that will turn on a dime and give you a nickel change and when the salesman "showed him the numbers" on it John

Peterson said, "There must be some mistake, I was looking to buy a mower from you, not your Mercedes."

"You get what you pay for," the salesman said.

And John said, "Well, you got that right. What I'm gonna get is a Snickers bar off your candy rack, and here's your 35¢." John went home and cleaned the spark plug on his puker and finished his mowing at a slow trot, which meant that the Snickers was calorie-free, and then some.

*   *   *   *   *   *   *   *   *   *

10 ON THIS DAY IN 1988 MINNESOTA BIGFOOT'S LETTER to the editor was sighted in the *Tribune*. He explained that he was leaving Minnesota and going to Canada because they would have more understanding there of a big hairy guy with body odor and a need for privacy. But if Minnesota could match their offer and provide him with a sanctuary, he might reconsider.

*   *   *   *   *   *   *   *   *   *

11 THE WALLEYE PHONE COMPANY WAS ESTABLISHED on this day in 1984 when Howie Humde strung a wire on two poles between his house and his sister's, across the alley in Bimpton.

*   *   *   *   *   *   *   *   *   *

12 ON THIS DAY IN 1986 OVID WEGDORN, WHOSE PLACE is three miles south of Mortwood and then a jag west, inquired in town about the cost of getting cable TV; his wife, Arlys, was fed up with watching a TV picture that was so snowy you couldn't even make out faces on "Days of Our Lives," and you had to see faces or it was nothing, she said. And it wasn't in color, because the leaves on the trees in the grove interfered with the signal from the tower fifty miles away.

It was better in winter—you could almost see details on two

channels with the rabbit ears up if you put some aluminum foil on the tips. It might have been slightly better with an aerial on the roof, but Ovid was against those. Dangerous.

The Go-No-Com Cable people told Ovid it was just a guess-timate, he should understand, but it could run him somewhere between $30,000 and $40,000 to bring cable to his farm.

Arlys never even considered asking for a satellite dish, because she knew what Ovid would say: "Those dishes are worse than antennas because they not only attract lightning they actually collect energy from a perfectly clear day and make their own lightning."

Sometimes she wondered if he wasn't as crazy as he looked. It was another one of those Minnesota marriages that only worked because there was compromise: she wished she didn't have to do it all though.

*   *   *   *   *   *   *   *   *   *

13 BILL MILLER WENT OUT INTO THE NINETY-EIGHT-degree heat of his backyard today in 1986 to test scientifically whether hot coffee cooled a guy off on a hot day. It was something his father had been saying for most of his eighty-eight years; Bill had been saying it himself for most of his fifty-seven years.

Bill sat on a lawn chair in the glaring sun with a thermal pot of steaming coffee beside him. He drank four cups of hot coffee, no cream, and took his temperature before he started and after the pot was empty; his body temperature had dropped two degrees. The remarkable thing was, he *felt* cooler too.

Come winter, Bill decided, he would go outside with a wet head and see if he got chilled and came down with a bad cold, which was something his mother had been saying for most of her eighty-one years.

*   *   *   *   *   *   *   *   *   *

14 HAROLD MIRE DECLARED ON THIS DAY IN 1975 THAT on the following day the family would eat only foods that occurred naturally on their acreage and did not walk on two or more legs. He mistakenly left out snakes, which offended his five-year-old daughter, who spent part of her summers catching snakes and giving them a vacation for a few hours in a large garbage can with their favorite snack foods. She also wanted to know if that meant they would be eating fried night-crawlers. No, he said, and even though the garden did look like a jungle now, it was also off limits during this important experiment.

*   *   *   *   *   *   *   *   *   *

15

HAROLD MIRE HAD ARISEN EARLY ON THIS DAY IN 1975 to forage for the family's breakfast, which consisted of:

chamomile tea
chopped dandelion greens (cooked in rainwater)
six black raspberries

The noon meal took all morning to prepare, and without his usual caffeine it was pretty much uphill for Harold:

chamomile tea (the edge of the driveway was full of it)
leftover dandelion greens
boiled Canadian thistle hearts garnished with elm leaves
wild rosehip jam on foxtail bread

Supper:

lamb's-quarter salad with chamomile dressing
Canadian thistle hearts wrapped in dandelion greens
chamomile tea
wild rosehip jam
foxtail bread

*   *   *   *   *   *   *   *   *   *

16

ON THIS DAY IN 1975 HAROLD MIRE AND FAMILY WOKE up hungry and drove to the Happy Chef restaurant in Boxelder.

Over a breakfast of eggs, ham, potatoes, toast, jelly, pancakes, juice, and coffee, Harold said, "It was a noble experiment. It proved that we could do it."

Ethel said, "If we do it again though, Harold, we need to find out what caused the hives." He said he was pretty sure it was the foxtail bread. It made his tongue hurt when he tried to eat it.

* * * * * * * * * * *

17

ON THIS DAY IN 1987 MINNESOTA BIGFOOT WAS sighted eating cake and ice cream at the fiftieth anniversary party of Maxine and Glenn Probbel. Glenn told Maxine that he thought it was probably Bob Truesdale's son. "You remember Bob—he lived across the alley from us in South St. Paul just after the war. Didn't we hear that one of his boys had some problems?"

* * * * * * * * * * *

18

JOHN AND DOROTHY VANDEBURGER OF RURAL BLUE Earth County—swept up in the dawn of the American camping movement on this day in 1966—set forth on their first camping trip after having purchased a Sears umbrella tent with external aluminum frame, a Coleman camp stove, two sleeping bags, a cooler, and thin aluminum eating-and-cooking equipment. "Won't it be fun to get away," John said.

The Vandeburgers were assigned to B-7 in Lot 4 of the Wonder Ridge Campground overlooking Carp River. It was an ideal spot if you liked a mixture of unusual odors, anthills, and Popsicle sticks. Boy, were they tired after they got the tent up. Boy, were they gonna sleep good. Boy, wasn't this the life. Look at those stars. But John couldn't even relax, let alone sleep, because the guy in B-6 was only fifteen feet away and snoring so dynamically his tent ropes vibrated. The young couple in B-8 spent the night in their tent engaged in one of the rites of marriage: they argued in hissing whispers.

The next morning, when John crawled out of the tent through the zippered opening, a woman was sitting at their picnic table shaving her legs. "I didn't think you'd mind—Benny is changing diapers on ours."

Later a man in his underwear—it looked like his anyway—walked past as John was pumping the stove up so he could fry bacon. "Put your thumb over the hole," the guy said.

When Dorothy returned from her trek to the pit toilet, she was visibly shaken and ashen and clutching her purse. That's when John climbed up on the picnic table and addressed the twenty or thirty families milling around within earshot: all their camping gear was up for sale, as is—you take down the poles, you roll up the bags, you fry the bacon. No reasonable offer refused. And none was.

* * *   *   *   *   *   * * *

19 METEOROLOGIST TERRY SLOOP WALKED THROUGH the courtyard at the Mississippi River Vista Minimum Security Prison in St. Paul this morning in 1986, circled the baseball diamond six times, and returned to his room to open the box his Aunt Therese had mailed. It contained a dozen ranger cookies, a scarf, a book of meditations and prayers by Reverend Ronnie Short, and a clipping from a newspaper about a man who had been shot three times in three years on his birthday by total strangers. Therese wondered what on earth this world was coming to. Terry didn't know. If he knew, he wouldn't be where he was for what he did, whatever that was.

* * *   *   *   *   *   * * *

20 IT WAS JUST ANOTHER DAY IN 1986 AT THE Mississippi River Vista Minimum Security Prison, much like yesterday except that Terry Sloop sat down at his desk to write to his three former wives right after breakfast. He was feeling generous. Terry wadded sheet after sheet and threw it toward the Care Bears wastebasket the prison auxiliary had given him at his one-year party. He was having trouble saying exactly what he meant to his first wife—and he had two more to go.

Finally he got down something that had a beautiful ring to it:
All is forgiven. I bear no ill will toward you.

He liked the economy of that effort so much that he decided
to send the same sentence to all three women, with "Dear Sweetie"
as the opener. They would love it. He still had the touch. He settled
on "Best Wishes" as the complimentary close.

He read the letters out loud one more time before sealing them:
sentimentality without maudlinity—the same goals he had set for
his ten o'clock weather report night after night. He picked a rabbit,
a deer, and a fox from his sheet of USPO 1st Class wildlife stamps.
He would drop by the post office on his way to Crafts. He would
finish his découpage serving tray today.

*   *   *   *   *   *   *   *   *   *

21

IT WAS THE NEXT DAY AT MISSISSIPPI RIVER VISTA
Minimum in 1986 when the old clock over the sink of Terry's two-
room efficiency showed it was tunneling time. He took off all his
clothes and hung them in the closet. He walked to the clothes
hamper at the door to the bathroom and took out the false bottom
and removed his tunneling uniform and put it on. Then he lifted
the rug in front of the TV set and pulled up the floor and climbed
into his excavation.

It was satisfying work gouging out dirt with the tablespoon and
putting it in his Twins cap and carrying it up to the bathtub. Later
that night he would haul it out to the garden and dump it, or if he
had to, wash it slowly down the drain. He estimated that he was
under the volleyball court by now. Of course he knew he could
just walk through the front gate—it didn't have a lock on it, just
a sign that said "Stone walls do not a minimum-security prison
make, nor iron bars a bungalow." But when he busted out of the
joint he wanted it to be a real escape that people would be talking
about for years. They'd be sorry they ever sent him there, but he
would bear them no ill will.

*   *   *   *   *   *   *   *   *   *

22

This Minnesota day is brought to you by HERB'S AC-UAUTO, the Midwest's only acupuncture garage, founded on this date in 1985, with one location to serve you, just off I-94 on Dale in St. Paul. Herb takes over when all the other mechanics throw up their hands, and he does it with a hammer and a sixteen-penny nail. He puts the nail on the pressure points of your car and then he hits the nail on the head to cure what ails your car. He won't treat your vehicle like some kind of mechanical object—he communicates with it and tries to understand your car's individual needs. And he doesn't care if you watch and drink a cup of herbal tea and participate in his diagnostic meditations. You won't find a better New Age mechanic anywhere.

*   *   *   *   *   *   *   *   *   *

23

ON THIS SUNNY DAY IN 1987, AS PART OF HIS continuing contract with Ethel to share the tedium, Harold Mire carried a basket of wash out to the clothesline and hoped that the traffic would be light on the road so nobody would drive by and see him. Harold was liberated—there was no question about that—but he was still slightly uneasy, especially on a weekday. Not everybody knew he was a self-employed entrepreneur with odd hours and that he put in his forty or fifty hours a week like a normal guy with normal everyday desires.

The feed truck went by. A couple of neighbors. He was able to duck down behind the tree. And then, as Harold was concentrating on shaking out a flannel bedsheet and folding it so it wouldn't drag on the ground when he pinned it up, he heard something coming up the lane. He was trapped: it was a Burlington Northern bus full of railroad workers. It was a liberated man's nightmare.

The driver rolled down the window and Harold walked over with the sheet in his hand. They needed directions, the driver said out the window. All the workers on Harold's side had their windows pulled down.

"I hang up the wash sometimes," Harold said.

"We can't understand you. Take the clothespins out of your mouth."

Harold gave the directions and with hand signals helped the driver turn around in the yard. The bus was rocking with good times all the way down the lane. Harold had made their day. From now on when it was his turn, he would hang the clothes up in the early morning under cover of dimness and bring them in at night. It was no more than any other red-blooded American man would do.

*　　*　　*　　　*　　　*　　　*　　　*　　　*　　*　　*

24

MINNESOTA BIGFOOT WAS SIGHTED IN AN ATHLETIC-supply store this day in 1987 getting a quote on some walking shoes. His feet were killing him—it was the concrete. The clerk told him that the Wonder Walker, with patented Rotator Insole and Rocket Toe, was the shoe he'd buy if he were in Bigfoot's shoes. In normal sizes it was on sale at $112.95. The salesman thought he could get Bigfoot into a size-25 super-wide on special order for $300. Bigfoot couldn't afford to ignore his feet, so he put a C-note down on the Wonder Walkers. In the meantime he bought a Swiss walking stick for $80.

*　　*　　*　　　*　　　*　　　*　　　*　　　*　　*　　*

25

IF YOU ARE PLANNING TO FLEE THE STATE TODAY, consider for a moment that this is the first day of the rest of your year. Face the music and tomorrow might be an improvement for once. It might not, too. But that's the chance we all take. Did you think life would be served up on a platter? And of course it would be better all the way around if you had the support of your family and the community and the people at work—but you can't have everything.

*　　*　　*　　　*　　　*　　　*　　　*　　　*　　*　　*

26

THE CRICKET SEASON IS IN FULL SWING TODAY AND
the crickets are coming out from under the baseboards, you can
hear them crawling in the walls, you find them in the sink in the
morning, in the light fixtures, in the washcloth, in the shower, in
your shoes.

It has come to choices now: Will you burn the house or will
you scream and start tearing down Sheetrock to get at them? Or
will you buy poison and spray it everywhere? Will you then cal-
culate (based on the one-ounce body weight of your hybrid crickets
that are killed by the fumes) what the effect might be on a creature
like yourself? Or will you hear the voice of reason and pounce on
the crickets with a Kleenex, roll them up, pinch them until the
brown gunk comes out, and then drop them in the wastebasket?

*　*　*　*　　*　*　*　*　*

27

ON THIS DAY IN 1985 ETHEL MIRE WAS THUMBING
through an issue of *Better Homes & Gardens* devoted to landscaping. She liked the looks of the little bridges over brooks and
the winding path through the flowers and the piles of rocks and
the swinging gates. She went out to the shop, where Harold was
changing brushes on the tractor generator, and asked him why they
couldn't do some landscaping and showed him the magazine.

"Just something else to mow around," he said. "A Chinese garden on this place would be like mammary glands on a boar."

Ethel had married Harold for some reason, but at the moment
she couldn't think of it. She knew it wasn't for his lapses into gross
humor.

"It doesn't have to be exactly like that—it could be something
different."

"We have something different—it took eighteen years to get it
right," Harold said. "I'd call it a unique yard that's restful to the
eyes, as they say in the landscaping business. And overflowing with
character."

These were the landscaping features he enumerated before Ethel cut him off and went back inside the house. He had hardly got started:

Dandelions, never sprayed—what's the point.
Pigeon grass.
Gopher mounds.
Thistles.
Smartweed.
Mole trails.
Clothesline with three poles.
Stumps.
Two and a half cars with perfectly good parts.
Dead elms.
Piles of branches.
Bricks from the old movie theatre.
A stack of steel fenceposts.
Compost heap.
Gravel driveway with corduroy ruts.
Boards from the old corncrib.
Chunks of sidewalk.
Trash burner.
Several 760-14 tires with some tread.
Twisted rain gutter.

* * * * * * * * *

28 ON THIS DAY IN 1986 DIRK D. BOLLATCH BROKE THE old record by eating the following foods at the Minnesota State Fair between 10:00 A.M. and 4:00 P.M., and afterward leaving the fairgrounds under his own power: soft pretzels (3), hard pretzels (8), hand-dipped caramels (14), pronto-pups (4), Middle Eastern pocket-puppies (2), snow cones (5), foot-long hot dogs (5), nacho-flavored soybean puffs (one-pounder bag), homemade french fries (88-ounce tub), bratwurst bugles (2), cotton candy (3), frosted maxi-donuts (1 dozen), chocolate-covered alfalfa pellets (12-ounce bale), needle noodles (1 swarm), and Blubber Bunnies (1½).

* * * * * * * * * *

29

BRUCE AND IRENE CHATSWORTH MET EACH OTHER
at Machinery Hill at the Minnesota State Fair on this day in 1986
and were married three days later. Irene had taken a lunch break
from her booth duties in Arts and Crafts and was sitting on a quiet
bench eating a pear and a cheese sandwich when a man sat down
beside her. He was wearing a cap with "Pioneer" printed above
the bill.

"I never get tired of looking at farm machinery," Bruce said.
"It's like being in church."

Eventually they stood up and walked together among the machines, Bruce giving a name to each machine. Hay baler, round
baler, end loader, manure spreader, Bobcat loader, swather, hay
conditioner, rake, drag, disc, combine, silage wagon, cultivator,
multi-weeder, field cultivator, chisel plow, moldboard plow,
sprayer, digger, stalk chopper, tractor, grain wagon, elevator, snow
blower, bush hog, sickle mower, silage chopper, planter, drill.

Every so often they would stop and Bruce would explain how
something worked. And then, over by the grain augers, they em-
braced. And kissed by the multi-weeder. Every year, they said,
they'd come back to Machinery Hill to relive the magic.

So far so good for Irene and her pioneer.

*   *   *   *   *   *   *   *   *

30

BIGFOOT WAS SIGHTED AT A FARM AUCTION IN
western Minnesota on this hot day in 1987 looking over the hayrack
of tools and miscellaneous. He bid 50¢ and got himself a cardboard
box containing old chisels, fabric samples, a bedpan, and lots of
miscellaneous in the bottom. Bigfoot then went over to the food
trailer and had himself two barbecues, a half-quart of warm Pepsi
(they had run out of ice), and a sack of candy corn.

After that feast he joined the crowd by the furniture. The auc-
tioneer was just saying that this bed wouldn't shake, rattle, or roll
and "Whatemabidfor" and "Somebodystartheroffforfivedollars."

Somebody did, and then somebody went up to $7.50, and that was
it. Things were going cheap, even Bigfoot was aware of that.

A steamer trunk from the old country went for $50. A dealer
got it—she'd turn around and sell it for three hundred bucks to
somebody from the Twin Cities. They were crazy up there for old
stuff to look at. But Bigfoot didn't know that. He thought the lady
was buying it to take a long ocean trip.

At that point Bigfoot paid the teller and walked into the grove
and then out again into the bean field, walking between rows until
he got to the Yellow Medicine River bank, whereupon he dangled
his big hairy hot feet in the water and sorted through his treasure
box.

*   *   *   *   *   *   *   *   *   *

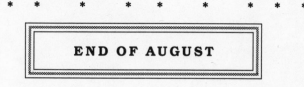

31 AT A DIG IN CENTRAL MINNESOTA ON THIS DAY IN
1983 an archaeologist uncovered a tire iron from 1948. It was found
inside a primitive wicker clothes basket from K Mart that also
contained some wet, moldy all-cotton towels carbon-dated to 1981,
and a Flintstones cup (circa 1958).

*   *   *   *   *   *   *   *   *   *

END OF AUGUST

SEPTEMBER

1 THE FIRST LEAF BLOWER WAS INVENTED ON THIS day in 1971. The critics said that there was no way the American public would ever shell out $200 for a gasoline-engine-powered machine whose whole function was to create a powerful wind for moving fallen leaves from one place to another in their yard. And besides, they said, hanging it on your shoulder to carry it was enough to cause a permanent limp. They were wrong about that, too: you stop walking funny a couple of days after using it, but your ears ring for a week.

*   *   *   *   *   *   *   *   *   *

2 TONIGHT IN 1986 HAROLD MIRE STOOD UP BEFORE going to bed and said to Ethel and Lily, "This concludes my portion of the broadcast day." Then he hummed the national anthem with a trumpet imitation, and threw in some streaking jets and explosions. He thought he was pretty darn funny. But when he tried it the next night, the majority of the family told him to cease and desist. There were two other phrases he was forbidden to utter within earshot of Lily and Ethel: (1) "If I lived alone . . ." as a preamble to how he would do a house-repair project and (2) "I rectum" as a yes answer to a question. They were cramping his style.

*   *   *   *   *   *   *   *   *   *

3 JANITOR MILO CHRISTENSEN WAS DOWN TO HIS LAST major job in preparation for the opening of classes in 1987 at Mortwood High School: something had to be done about the rusty troll on the front lawn. Heber Rogno, folk artist, had created it the past summer, mostly out of eighth-of-an-inch steel plate, with a tie-rod end for the nose, brake pedals for the ears, and steel shavings for hair. The eyes were two ball bearings. Milo Christensen, folk janitor, had a few ideas of his own.

* * * * * * * * * *

4 AT THE OFFICIAL UNVEILING AND DEDICATION ceremony today folk artist Heber Rogno explained to the students and faculty how the troll as it had rusted had become more and more the mysterious creature of Scandinavia, a symbol of the wildness in us all that wanted to get out and dance around. The school superintendent did not like the sound of that so early in the year, but he untied the rope anyway and took the tarp off a shiny, cheerful troll painted the same color as the Home Ec room. It looked like the symbol of the tiny shoe-salesman in us all trying to get out.

Heber spent a week sandblasting himself and the troll back into the dark world of the unconscious.

* * * * * * * * * *

5 This Minnesota day is sponsored by BULK BOOKS, the big books for big readers. Next time you go into your favorite bookstore or gas station, look for the BULK display and you'll get a wide choice of really big books with lots of pages. If titles don't matter to you but heft does, then BULK BOOKS have your name written all over them. If you aren't getting over a thousand pages of print per book, you need BULK. There's more book for your buck with BULK BOOKS.

* * * * * * * * * *

6 ON THIS DAY IN 1983 HAROLD WAS SCRAPING THE chipped paint off the siding on the house board by board to prepare it for new paint. He was on the east side of the house and had just moved the extension ladder over and was climbing steadily up it.

But for all his efforts, his head remained at the level where he could look into the kitchen through the little window over the sink and see Ethel doing the dishes.

Ethel knew how much Harold hated painting and scraping, so it seemed natural for him to take time out for some impromptu entertainment for her; she thought he was doing a fairly good pantomime of a man climbing a ladder.

Harold jumped off the ladder when only the top three rungs were visible. The ladder was disappearing into the ground. He had read about things like this happening to the other guy. Now he was that guy. He was also that guy who pulled the ladder back out and then got down on his belly and inched over to the hole and peered in. It was deep and it went way back under where he was lying, so he inched back and thought of all the worst possibilities, including that they had staked the horse out there to graze just yesterday.

Harold went inside and called Mark the Backhoe Genius: if Mark couldn't do it with a backhoe, nobody could. What he did for Harold was dig down and find the two culprits that had created the sinkhole in the yard. It was a double whammy, he said. First it was an old wooden septic tank, made from redwood. It had collapsed finally. But the other thing was the '37 Chevy that had been buried there as the replacement.

After Mark had peeled the top off the Chevy, he and Harold were afraid to look too close inside it. They expected to see a human skeleton behind the wheel, but they didn't. The skeleton was in the back seat and it had once belonged to a complete groundhog. They filled the car with field rocks and covered it up.

"What are the damages?" Harold said.

"How does forty bucks sound?" Mark said.

"It sounds like the bargain of the day," Harold said. He paid Mark in cash and didn't get a receipt. They were both part of the economic underground.

*   *   *   *   *   *   *   *   *   *

7 ON THIS OPENING DAY OF CLASSES IN 1987 AT Prairie Gate College, Minnesota Bigfoot took a seat in the back row of Grammar and Composition, a freshman requirement and Bigfoot's first college class.

The teacher came in carrying a file folder and the three required books. He stood at the front and said, "I have been teaching freshman English for twenty-five years now. Every year I have given the same advice as the class starts: *If you can't write clearly in your native language you are handicapped, and if you don't enjoy reading you have cut yourself off from one of the supreme pleasures of the world.* I am giving you the same advice, but instead of continuing with you for the semester in the role of teacher in this punishing charade of having you hand in papers and read assignments, I am walking back out the door and to the parking lot, where I will climb into my '78 Ford and drive home. Ladies and gentlemen: So long. It's been nice knowing you."

Bigfoot stood up and left as well. His career as a nontraditional student had turned sour before it started.

*　　*　　*　　*　　*　　*　　*　　*　　*

8 ON THIS DAY IN 1987 TWIN CITIES ENTREPRENEUR Seward L. Tupte threw wide the doors of his Dressing for Defeat store in St. Paul. After starting several other businesses that had gone belly up, Seward had become interested in helping those like himself find an appropriate dressing style. "If you are a big flop in life," he said at the ribbon-cutting ceremony, "try dressing for defeat. Let's face it, very few of us ever succeed. If you never climb to the pinnacle and instead take one major nosedive after another, you'll look completely ridiculous in successful clothes. I know I did. All I'm saying is, if your goal is to just make it through life without being noticed all that much, try dressing for defeat. We can't all be winners."

*　　*　　*　　*　　*　　*　　*　　*　　*

9 SEWARD L. TUPTE DECLARED BANKRUPTCY ON THIS day in 1987. As CEO of the Dressing for Defeat store, he listed as assets twenty-five racks of brown clothes and an empty cash register.

*　　*　　*　　*　　*　　*　　*　　*　　*

10

ON THIS DAY IN 1986 BURTON DADE FOUND OUT again that farming is a spectator sport and that no matter how hard you try, if you make a mistake farming, it's public, at least until somebody invents a Stealth line of machinery. If something goes wrong, it usually does it while your neighbor is driving by in the pickup with a notepad and binoculars. Say the wheel comes off of your John Deere 4420 in the middle of the field—which Burton's did—and just stands there for all the world to see:

"Yeah, that wheel was just out there in the middle of the field and Burton was still moving. A lotta guys'd look back more often than that."

The average time until the news of your mistake is all over the township is three hours. The average time until the mistake is forgotten is equal to Burton Dade's lifetime.

*   *   *   *   *   *   *   *   *   *

11

ON THIS DAY IN 1986 JUST AS TWO NEW SHOPPING malls opened in the Twin Cities, breaking the old record of one opening in a single day, a study by a team of experts revealed that if you laid all the shops in all the malls in the Metro Area end to end they would reach the South Dakota border, but business wouldn't be much worse.

*   *   *   *   *   *   *   *   *   *

12

TODAY IN 1987 THE GOPHER FAIRNESS IN BATHROOMS commission issued the following guidelines for describing bathroom size and utility in houses for sale:

Double bath: a shower, tub, sink, toilet, vanity, dressing room, VCR, and phone.
Single bath: either shower or tub, sink, and toilet.

¾ bath: toilet and sink.

½ bath: toilet.

¼ bath: if you either have to shake the handle or reach inside the tank and fiddle with something to keep the toilet from running.

⅛ bath: if the bolts are loose on the bottom of the toilet.

1/16 bath: if the water always rises right to the rim of the bowl when you flush it.

1/32 bath: if the water rises to the rim whenever the neighbors flush their toilet.

1/64 bath: coffee can with lid.

*   *   *   *   *   *   *   *   *   *

13

ON THIS DAY IN 1953 WHEN HAROLD MIRE WAS thirteen years old, two things happened to him that he said he would never in his life ever forget even if he lived to be a hundred. But he forgot both things before he was twenty. And in 1988 he couldn't even remember the general subject area or whether the incidents had involved crippling humiliation or just your everyday failure, like so much that he *could* remember.

*   *   *   *   *   *   *   *   *   *

14

ON THIS DAY IN 1971 ROTAN B. DRONBERG, THE talking mime from Waseca, began entertaining his co-workers at the overstuffed-furniture plant with imitations of domestic pets and supervisors.

*   *   *   *   *   *   *   *   *   *

15

ON THIS DAY IN 1972, EXACTLY A YEAR AND A DAY after he was fired from the furniture plant, Rotan B. Dronberg changed his name to Jake Dronberg and then to Barry Crocker and landed an early-morning announcing job on fledgling Gopher State Radio.

"Betty's Brother" originated from the studio in the men's rest room, which was convenient for Barry but not for anybody else. The salmonella outbreak among the administrative staff from bad tuna sandwiches almost killed his show in its third week, for reasons that need not be spelled out. If that kind of stuff interests you, check the newspapers.

*   *   *   *   *   *   *   *   *   *

16

ON THIS DAY IN 1975 GOPHER STATE RADIO personality Barry Crocker fell head first into his top-loading washing machine out at his trailer home near the transmitter. He sustained several bruises and abrasions during the spin cycle, but refused treatment.

*   *   *   *   *   *   *   *   *   *

17

ON THIS DAY IN 1979 GOPHER STATE RADIO personality Barry Crocker began wearing a shower cap, raincoat, and rubber gloves so people wouldn't recognize him when he appeared in public.

*   *   *   *   *   *   *   *   *   *

18

THIS WAS THE DAY IN 1983 WHEN HAROLD MIRE arrived for his week at the Passive Energy Camp for Men, in the woods north of Duluth. (Ethel had signed him up because she thought it would be good for him.) By midmorning Harold, along with seventy other men, had already pretended to be a small animal (Harold picked pocket gopher) and had watched a Theatre of Maleness repertory company enact the arrival of puberty in leotards.

After the noon bag-lunch of pita bread and brown paste, he did breathing exercises and then some guy read nature poems. Before supper he hugged a tree and then drew a circle around himself in the dirt and tried to project himself into the universe. After supper, when it was his turn to share an important feeling at the campfire, he told them that he felt he got over 150,000 miles out of his used cars because he performed daily inspection and maintenance. You had to stay on top of it, he said.

Later that night he got up from his bunk without disturbing any of the other guys (they were wiped out from their day of passivity anyway), rolled up his sleeping bag, walked to the parking lot, and headed home. The '70 Chrysler didn't miss a beat. It made him feel like a king until he started thinking about what he would say to Ethel and what animal he would be when he did it.

* * * * * * * * * *

19

THIS IS CELLAR AWARENESS DAY IN MINNESOTA. Remember to go to your cellar when tornadoes threaten, but be sure to take a flashlight and shine it around a lot during your stay to keep the spiders at bay, and the salamanders, box-elder bugs, sow bugs, mice, centipedes, and those half-dollar-size things that can jump almost four feet horizontally if they detect body heat. Wear shoes.

* * * * * * * * * *

20

ON THIS DAY IN 1987 A LETTER FROM MINNESOTA Bigfoot to the editor was sighted in the *Star-Tribune:*

> *Where I come from we don't wear clothes and I'm not about to start now just because some repressed individuals signed a petition. I scare fewer people than a high school principal or a fully clothed lawyer. And another thing: enormous eyebrows are not a crime in this state.*

It was widely assumed by the public that the letter was written by a disgruntled Minnesota celebrity, not Bigfoot.

* * * * * * * * * *

21

ON THIS CLEAR DAY IN 1987 AT 10:00 IN THE morning, Henry Longacre was in the northeast corner of his compound cutting down some errant flora with his armored Snapper riding mower. The big question as always for Henry Longacre was not whether somebody was after him: it was *who*, and *when*, and *how*. He tried to cover all the bases.

At 10:01 Henry's million-dollar security system failed to adequately protect his spacious fort and house north of Anoka.

This is what happened: The orbit of France's Pomme de Terre communications satellite had decayed rapidly, and upon re-entry, several pieces exceeding one ton in weight peppered Henry's complex. A two-ton chunk, for instance, had turned Henry's house into a crater.

The general alarm did not go off. The iron gates did not drop over the window of his reinforced-concrete earth home. The automatic dialer on the phone did not dial 911 or the National Guard or the FBI at the first sign of trouble. Even the feather in Henry's security cap, the wide-perimeter multiphase early-warning sensor system in the fields around his house, was caught with its rear end hanging out; it never made so much as a peep or a whimper before it was transformed to nondigital, smoking silicone rubble.

It was over in seconds. After Henry had cleaned the grime from his glasses, he stood up to survey the damage and set off the only remaining security device, the shrieking motion-detector, which Henry promptly disabled by beating it with the stub end of the steering-wheel shaft from his twisted Snapper. This left him completely defenseless, the way he was when he was born, except that he was now wearing the right sleeve of a Jordache sweatshirt, part of a Reebok athletic sock, and the waist portion of his Banana Republic pants minus the fly.

At that moment, the Pizza Hut van drove up with a large sausage-and-pepperoni. Henry's automatic dialer had done its best before it expired.

*   *   *   *   *   *   *   *   *

22 AT NOON ON THIS DAY IN 1983 BEFORE GOING OUT to pick apples from the two trees that were more than ready, Harold Mire went into the cellar to count the remaining stock of quart jars of applesauce. There were sixty-seven quarts from 1981 (down from 127), thirty-four quarts from 1982, and twelve unlabeled quarts that looked like they might be from 1914—he would put on his coveralls and hard hat with goggles to dump those on the compost heap. If they were real bad, he would shoot them with the .22 rifle from a distance. You can't be too careful.

That meant 101 quarts had to be scheduled for consumption— or roughly two per week for a family of three, which wasn't cruel and unusual applesauce-eating, but he had found that there were some weeks when they couldn't look applesauce in the face, so that meant they would have to increase their intake the following weeks to stay on schedule. And that could snowball fast. It was one of those homesteading problems that gnawed at you in the middle of the night and cast a shadow over the good life.

*   *   *   *   *   *   *   *   *   *

23 HAROLD MIRE'S THIRTY-YEAR-OLD NEPHEW TOBY stopped by the place today in 1987 on his way from Pennsylvania to Huron, where he had business to conduct. It was his first visit to the stomping grounds of his eccentric uncle. Harold's sister-in-law, Grace, had obviously told him to do it.

Harold set Toby up with the deluxe Mire overnight package, which included a sleeping assignment in "the shed," a little building south of the house. As Harold says, it has all the amenities: door, window, roof, floor, walls, a pull-out bed, and an unobstructed seven-mile view of the cultivated plains.

Toby had struck it rich in something that involved reselling mortgages or mortuaries—Harold had missed it—and had already mentioned twice in the first hour of his stay that his house in Pittsburgh had six bathrooms: one per family member and two for backup. Harold told him not to use the word "backup." He told

Toby that the shed had no bathroom, but it was an easy two
hundred yards to the two-holer behind the apple tree. But why
bother, Harold said, when Toby could just walk to the edge of the
field to shake the dew off his lily.

"What?" Toby said.

"You know, take a whiz. Drain your snake."

He forgot to tell Toby he shouldn't slam the door on the shed
or the latch on the outside would catch and he would be stuck
inside. Harold had been meaning to fix that.

*   *   *   *   *   *   *   *   *   *

24

TOBY WASN'T UP FOR OATMEAL AND TOAST WITH
Harold and Ethel on this day in 1987 but they figured sleeping
late was about par for somebody with six bathrooms and a line of
work that couldn't be explained to the common man or woman.
When Ethel went out to dump the biodegradables on the compost
heap at 10:30, she saw Toby's scrawled sign in the window of the
shed: "HELP!!" Ethel unlatched the door. Toby went past her at a
high rate of speed to the outhouse, and then went straight to his
Lincoln without saying a word.

Harold later wrote a small note to Toby's mother that outlined
the unusual nature of her son's visit and enclosed the "Help!!" sign
in Toby's hand as a souvenir.

*   *   *   *   *   *   *   *   *   *

25

ON THIS DAY IN 1984 HAROLD MIRE SAW THE SHEET
of cafeteria rules his daughter had brought home from school:

1. The purpose of eating is to fuel the body. The high school
   cafeteria is a fuel depot not a game room. You're not down
   there to have a good time.
2. The line forms at the rear. Don't crowd, push, jockey, jump,
   slide, climb the walls, remove clothes, whistle, dance, practice oriental warfare, or try to communicate with the dead.
3. Loud talking is discouraged before, during, and after eating.

Laughter is forbidden at all times, because people could think you were laughing at them. There's a place for laughter and that's when something is funny.

4. You are provided with only a blunt spoon because forks and knives are dangerous. All hard foods are cooked until they are soft enough to eat with a spoon. Don't bend the spoon or use it as a catapult. Don't balance the spoon on your nose.

5. Don't play with your food. Don't talk with your mouth full. Don't expectorate your food against the wall if it doesn't suit your taste. Don't dawdle. Don't read books and eat. Don't push your food around on the plate. Don't mix separate items of food together, such as canned corn and FDA boiled-beef cubes.

6. Don't glare at the food monitors—they're just doing their job, which is to tap you on the head or pull your ears when you slow down the fueling process or behave in a manner inappropriate for rational human beings in a feeding situation.

7. Return your spoon, plate, and tin cup to the designated area. Don't sail the plate in through the hole. Don't stomp on the cup.

8. You have five minutes to eat.

9. This is an educational institution. Act like an adult and you'll be treated like one. But if you act like a child, we'll win, because we know every single one of your devious and childish tricks, and don't you forget it.

After Harold read the cafeteria rules he told his daughter that he thought the main reason we had fought World War II was to stop that sort of thing. He asked her what she thought. She said she didn't think anything when it came to school. "After ten years you finally get used to it," she said.

"Have they got other rules?" he said.

"Eighty pages. It's thick. I never did let you see it. Mom said it wouldn't be healthy for you. Especially the library rules."

"Try me," Harold said.

"Well, the first library rule is you aren't allowed to use the school library if you have low grades or misbehave, because the library is a privilege, not a right."

"Interesting. See, honey, I'm talking in a normal voice. I suppose you thought if I saw some of those rules I'd assemble a com-

mando assault team and go into that brick prison and try to restore
freedom and the American way of life, huh?"

"Let me handle it, Dad. It's no big deal. It's just school."

*   *   *   *   *   *   *   *   *   *

26

ON THIS NIGHT IN 1985 MINNESOTA BIGFOOT WAS
sighted in the Rhino Room of the Starburst Hotel in St. Paul with
a group of people who had turned in their personal invitation at
the door and received a meat-loaf dinner, a set of steak knives,
and a golf hat for consenting to watch a beautiful video presentation
on a luxurious resort complex to be built as soon as enough shrewd
investors signed a contract for a choice lot and paid some money
down. Before he started the show, Mr. Delaney, a striking individual with a necklace, five rings, and two suntans, mentioned that
the marsh had been drained and the staking and grading were
almost completed. The audience applauded.

The video featured many smiling couples with no cares walking
arm in arm through hundreds of flower gardens west of Duluth,
with orchestra music in the background. After Mr. Delaney had
turned the lights back on and grabbed the hand-held microphone
and begun explaining time-sharing, Bigfoot was out the door with
his golf hat and steak knives, having separated the wheat from the
chaff.

*   *   *   *   *   *   *   *   *   *

27

"MY BELIEF IN SERIAL MONOGAMY ALSO APPLIES TO
cars," Harold said to his writer friend on this day in 1987 as they
stood around waiting for a farm auction to begin. "It's best to find
a car you love and stay with it until one or the other of you is
ready to be pushed into the grove for decoration." Harold meant
it, but he had dressed it up a little for his author pal in case he
was short on material.

But the fact was that when Harold was young and in his prime
driving years, monogamy was the last thing on his mind, and some
of the best cars that passed his way were now nowhere to be seen.

He was loyal to their memory, though, whatever that was worth.

In 1956, the summer after Harold's high-school graduation, his father had given him the family's '42 Plymouth coupe after he had traded up to a Ford. Harold then proceeded to drive the wheels off of it. He couldn't even remember where it went after he had cooked the engine in 1957 or so. He had probably abandoned it like so much metal.

Harold's earliest memory of the '42 Plymouth was an incident in 1942, or was it '43? Or did he remember it? It was hard to remember if he remembered it or not. His Uncle Henry had taken the Plymouth for a test run before he boarded the train to go off to be a paratrooper. He went into that S-curve on U.S. 14 south of Fremson at ninety-seven miles an hour. It shimmied a little, he said, but when he reached the second part of the S, where many a car before it had left the road and ended up in the Britmans' yard or barn, the speedometer was pegged and it held the road like a tank.

"It's a good one," he told Harold's dad. "I hope you've still got it when I come back. I hope I come back."

He did come back, and Harold's dad still had it when he did.

Harold's happiest recollection of the Plymouth was this day in 1949, when he was ten years old. The whole family was on the way to visit relatives—what else—when the needle of the temperature gauge disappeared to the right and a cloud of steam shot out from under the hood.

"What the Sam Hill?" his dad said. It was a rhetorical question; he pretty much knew what the Sam Hill: it was one of two things. It turned out not to be a split radiator hose. It was the second thing: frost plug. A frost plug had corroded and popped out of the engine block and all the coolant had disappeared on the road.

Harold watched his dad work on the car while his mother watched the other kids throw rocks in the creek. His dad found a stick and whittled it down to size and tapped it into the engine block and refilled the radiator with creek water, and they were ready to roll again. The wooden plug stayed in until the fall, when his dad put in a metal model and replaced the creek water with Prestone.

That frost-plug performance by his father might have been the seed of Harold's own joy in repairs: finding out what was wrong was half the fun and the other half was fixing it with whatever was handy.

*   *   *   *   *   *   *   *   *   *   *

28

BIRTHDAY OF OMAR PIMMELSON, WHO WAS GOVERNOR-
elect of Minnesota for thirty-six hours, the shortest such tenure in
Gopher State history. The Minnesota Code forbids the publication
of the exact date, but a loophole in the laws allows you to know
that Omar was asked to step down after it was determined that he
had intended to enter the lutefisk-joke competition in St. Paul, not
run for the highest office in the state; he had been given the wrong
entry forms by the official in charge of both contests.

After the election Omar slept like a log for thirteen hours. Then
he was awake for fourteen hours, but he was groggy and drank
quite a bit of coffee. And then he slept again until his aide woke
him up to tell him that he was out on his ear.

For a detailed account of Governor Pimmelson's brief but calm
reign as governor-elect, see the massive *Glory Day and a Half*, by
history professor Siever Olson, where you can learn that Omar was
from South Dakota, had lived in Iowa, last voted in North Dakota,
and liked bullheads better than walleyes. But you have to say this
for Omar, he could tell a story: his collection of lutefisk jokes has
outsold Professor Olson's biography almost a hundred to one.

*   *   *   *   *   *   *   *   *   *

29

HAROLD'S SISTER CAROLE CALLED HIM OVER TO HER
house today in 1988 to take care of an electrical problem that had
been bothering her for two years. The wall switch outside the back
door was a double: the one switch turned the basement light on
and off, but the other switch did nothing. "If it does nothing,"
Harold said, "then you're home free."

"I don't like a switch that does nothing but looks like it does,"
Carole said. "It either has to do something or be taken out."

Harold removed the plate and tested the wires. Apparently the
nothing-switch used to do something, probably turn on the porch
light. It was hot when the other switch was on, so he clipped the
wires and made it dead and put the cover back on.

"The switch is still there," Carole pointed out.

"Yeah, but now it really does do nothing."

"But it looks like it does."

Harold removed the plate again and took out the do-nothing switch, taped the wires, put the plate back on, and put a piece of masking tape over the hole where the switch handle had stuck through.

"Good," Carole said. "Now it looks like it does nothing."

"It looks like crap if you ask me," Harold said.

*   *   *   *   *   *   *   *   *   *

30

THIS AFTERNOON IN 1987 HAROLD MIRE HAD planned to straighten up the shop and take a couple of layers of stuff off the workbench, but the mailman put a stop to that by delivering a brown envelope from his mother. It was more stuff she had saved over the years and was now packing up and sending off to the kids in regularly scheduled shipments. Today it was all of Harold's report cards from kindergarten through sixth grade.

The way Harold remembered it, he had been a good little worker in the grades, and the perfect victim. But the "Reports of Progress" had some surprises for him. The notes the teachers consistently wrote in the "Remarks" box were all similar to the one from second grade: "Harold visits too much with his neighbors."

Harold knew he liked visiting with his neigbhbors as an adult. If somebody dropped by he was more than willing to talk till the cows came home. But he thought he had been a loner as a kid, that he had learned to be sociable. Apparently he had been pretty good at it in grade school, only it was bad to do it. Now it was okay, mainly. Sometimes when Ethel came home from substitute-teaching she would ask him what he did all day, and he would say, "Jack came by." No elaboration was necessary: Harold had visited with his neighbor too much and didn't get anything done.

Harold received only I's, which meant "improving but not yet satisfactory," in "Uses health information in daily living." Nails and teeth were checked by the teacher as the main offenders. Well, he had kept improving on the teeth situation—he now brushed once a day unless he forgot. But his nails presently hovered between an L ("less satisfactory than last quarter") and a U ("unsatisfactory"). You work on cars and machinery and you get grease under your fingernails. Maybe for a wedding he would use a toothpick and then scrub them with a vegetable brush, but otherwise he still thought—as he had in his formative years, evidently—that dirt under the nails was nothing to get upset about.

But of the thirty or so categories of evaluation, it was "Learning to carry a tune with others" that surprised him. It was all U's, for seven years. He remembered opening the songbooks with everybody else, and he remembered the teacher strumming on the autoharp, and he even remembered singing at the top of his voice on "My Bonnie Lies over the Ocean" and "Long, Long Ago." But his grades indicated that he should have moved his lips without making any noise during Music.

As an adult Harold would sometimes chord on the piano and sing. Now that he thought about it, Ethel and Lily usually went out to weed the garden or scrape ice off the walks when he executed what he had always assumed was singing but was apparently nothing more than tuneless bellowing.

In only one category did Harold get an S every reporting period: "Is free from evidence of overfatigue." Harold was no longer satisfactory on that count; he often felt overfatigued before he got out of bed in the morning. And today he was overfatigued from reading his "Reports of Progress."

*   *   *   *   *   *   *   *   *

END OF SEPTEMBER

OCTOBER

1 ON THIS DAY IN 1948 THE FIRST MICROWAVE OVEN was tested in Minnesota by inventor Corwin Pithrode. After a fifteen-second burst, the hamburger patty he had placed on the rack was still pink and cold, but everything else on the kitchen counter had been cooked to a frazzle, including Corwin's cowhide billfold and the handle of his screwdriver. It was back to the drawing board.

* * * * * * * * * *

2 HAVING MADE SOME ADJUSTMENTS ON THE EMISSION tube of his microwave prototype this morning in 1948, Corwin Pithrode placed an ordinary cup of cold water in the oven and turned on the switch. In two minutes the water was boiling!!! He was ecstatic. He imagined a future in 1988 where every home had a microwave oven and people didn't just use them to warm up leftovers, they cooked with recipe books written for the microwave, and they bought special containers and utensils!!! The people of 1988 would save so much time they could go on long vacations in their hovercraft!!!! He woke his wife up to tell her about the incredible profits they would make from his four-hundred-pound electronic marvel that made the lights dim and drove the cockroaches crazy.

What Corwin didn't know was that when he had heated the water for his teabag in the microwave oven he had also set fire to his neighbors' garage and neutered their prize poodle.

* * * * * * * * * *

3 BIRTHDAY OF MELVIN PITTCAIRN, THE INVENTOR of the Sneeze Helmet.

First came the salad, then the salad bar, the greatest advance in salad delivery since the the Pilgrims landed with a hold full of head lettuce and croutons, and a bilge full of house dressing.

Then came the salad-bar Sneeze Guard, the very attractive plastic deflector shield that prevents over 80 percent of the accidental intrusions of unwanted particulates into the chilled fixings. And then came the *coup de salade* in salad-bar protection: the Sneeze Helmet, with its personal oxygen supply and scientifically designed flip-up mouth flap for easier dining. Wear it a few times and you'll think you were born with it.

Look for these comforting words on the window of your favorite restaurant: "Sneeze Helmets issued here."

*   *   *   *   *   *   *   *   *   *

4 **This day is brought to you by GARY'S GAME FISH CAFE,** fifty years in the same location, straddling the border between Iowa and Minnesota. Serving the finest in game-fish novelties, including Walleye Whoopies, Organic Carp Chips, Crappie Tater Toots, Pike Pâté, and (only on the Iowa side) Boiled Bullhead Bits in a Bag.

*   *   *   *   *   *   *   *   *   *

5 ON THIS DAY IN 1981 THE FIRST SIX-FIGURE advance for a novel about duck hunting was handed over to Minnesota author George Peterson, who cashed his $1,026.73 check for *Shoot or Go Blind*.

*   *   *   *   *   *   *   *   *   *

6 ON THIS DAY IN 1972 THE FIRST HOME-entertainment center was manufactured in Minnesota. The critics said there was no way you could get the American public to buy cheap-looking furniture whose whole purpose was to hold a TV set and all the other junk that went with it. But they were wrong— which is why they are critics and the rest of us are consumers.

*   *   *   *   *   *   *   *   *   *

7

This Minnesota day has been purchased by NATIONAL AMERICAN TUBING, the world's largest supplier of valves, fittings, pipes, and bushings. So next time you think tubing, think NATIONAL AMERICAN, the company that cares about you, the little guy who's just trying to make ends meet. If you don't seem to be having much fun lately, or you lost your job and then your car broke down and the stress aggravated your health problems, NATIONAL AMERICAN TUBING is there to lean on. Stay right by the phone because they'll be calling soon to check on you.

* * * * * * * * * *

8

ON THIS DAY IN 1987 JOSEPH T., A RESIDENT OF Bloomington, bought a Maxi-Pro metal detector for $678.99, figuring a guy might as well get the best one while he's at it. You buy a cheap anything and what've you got? Besides Joe was interested in serious detecting of precious metals and meant to supplement his income at first and then eventually become independently wealthy and quit his job. As long as he was at it, he bought himself the Professional Excavation Kit, in a Gore-Tex carrying case with belt loop, containing a titanium coin probe with pearl handle and a high-nickel stainless-steel Finder's Trowel with compass and thermometer for an additional $179.98.

* * * * * * * * * *

9

ON HIS WAY HOME FROM WORK ON THIS NEXT DAY in 1987 Joseph T. bought the Magno-Shield Metal-Pro coveralls with the nonconductive fly that would not throw off your delicate detector calibrations. They were marked down to $99.99—he bought two pairs, because one pair could be at the cleaners while he wore the clean pair on detector expeditions. He also bought a pair of Pro-Search shoes, so it would be clear that he was a journeyman treasure hunter and not one of your Sunday hobbyists with the $30 toys. In the evening, when Joe T. told his wife how much the whole ball of metal-detecting wax had set him back, he shaved six hundred bucks off, but she still went into the bedroom and slammed the door. "It's an investment in the future," he said through the door.

* * * * * * * * * *

10

JOSEPH T. SPENT THIS DAY IN 1987 READING THE manual for his Maxi-Pro metal detector and learning about his discrimination filter, his automatic ground balance, and his threshold knob. He asked his wife to shorten the legs on the Magno-Shield coveralls, because the cuffs tended to catch on the soles of his Pro-Search shoes and cause unprofessional stumbling. He was forced to do it himself and got the left leg way shorter than the right, but his calf-length Pro-Search socks took up the slack.

* * * * * * * * * *

11

UP AT DAWN ON THIS DAY IN 1987 JOSEPH T. WENT forth on his first expedition, traveling around the two-acre vacant lot behind his house, and by dark had found sixteen items of value: three copper coins, one nickel, one quarter, a Lone Ranger Ring (value unknown), four pre-1970 aluminum beer cans ("You don't see those much anymore"), one sardine can (with attached key and rolled top) probably from the '50s (he would have to look it up to be sure of the date), one 1963 South Dakota license plate, two cast-iron skillets (found together—strange), one paring knife with the point broken off, and one large brooch encrusted with diamonds that spelled out "Souvenir of Baxter Bullhead Derby."

* * * * * * * * * *

12

MINNESOTA BIGFOOT WAS SIGHTED WALKING OUT of *Top Gun* this evening in 1987 and demanding his money back.

The management of Theatre-8 accommodated him after he lifted
the ticket booth off its foundation. Bigfoot did not like movies that
insulted his intelligence, but he guessed he was in the minority.
The place had been packed—which was another thing he didn't
like.

* * * * * * * * * *

13

AN AWFUL ODOR EMANATING FROM SOMEPLACE
down on the main floor on this day in 1987 had greeted Carol and
Tom Nooley, St. Paul, as they woke up. It had crept under their
door in the night. They conducted an abbreviated sniff search
before they left for work. Tom thought it was the drain in the
basement and so he put a Danish Modern dinner plate over it until
later.

* * * * * * * * * *

14

THE ODOR DIDN'T SEEM TOO BAD WHEN CAROL AND
Tom came home yesterday evening in 1987, but then this morning
it had enough molecules in it to set off the smoke alarm in the
kitchen. They thought about it all day at work and Tom came up
with the dishwasher.

"Remember when I cooked the halibut steaks in the dishwasher? Maybe some of it fell down behind that thing in the back."

He was right. After some Top Job and scraping, Tom and Carol
celebrated with a glass of white wine and went to bed.

* * * * * * * * * *

15

CAROL AND TOM GOT UP IN AN ATMOSPHERE SO
thick they could cut it with a knife on this day in 1987. They took
the battery out of the smoke alarm. They called in sick and
launched a major sniff offensive, concentrating on the refrigerator.
The green pepper had turned to a whitish-greenish liquid, but its

odor was retained fairly well by the Baggie, at least until Tom
broke it. Item by item, they removed the contents of the refrigerator. A Tupperware dish was filled with something they didn't
recognize—it might have been chip dip from the Christmas party
two years before. Finally they pulled out that little tray under the
refrigerator they didn't know was there until they had got down
with their faces on the floor and peered in. On the tray were four
rotten potatoes with three dead mice that had burrowed in and
expired somehow in their little Idaho Russet homes. Victory.

*   *   *   *   *   *   *   *   *   *

16

HOWIE HUMDE HIRED HIS OLD FRIEND MACK ON
this day in 1985 as the troubleshooter for Walleye Phone Company.
Howie and Mack went way back to the Vo-Tech days. Mack vol-
unteered his pickup as part of the handshake deal and painted the
company logo on the driver's side: a ten-pound jumping walleye
with a phone receiver in its mouth.

*   *   *   *   *   *   *   *   *   *

17

ON THIS DAY IN 1985 HOWIE HUMDE HIRED TOOTIE,
Mack's girlfriend, to do the billing for Walleye Phone Company
and to run the switchboard. Mack, Tootie, and Howie then had a
meeting and voted to make themselves the board of directors, after
which they set several company policies, the most important of
which was:

For better or worse, we will not take any guff from anybody.
Life is too short.

*   *   *   *   *   *   *   *   *   *

18

THIS IS AS GOOD A DAY AS ANY TO WARN YOU DUCK
hunters to be on the lookout when the season opens. The sad fact

is that every year since 1983 a few sick individuals have gone out
to the sloughs, swamps, lakes, and marshes of Minnesota and have
erected life-size human decoys that from a distance look exactly
like duck hunters, but in reality are nothing but stuffed dummies
in camouflage clothes carrying wooden guns and a fifth of colored
water. It's enough to make a grown man cry to think how many of
you dedicated duck hunters will get up in the dark on the damp,
cold morning of the opener to lash your duckboats to the top of
your pickups, and then drive out to your special spot only to find
it already occupied—or so it seems.

And then on you drive, around and around, sadder and sadder,
looking for a place to take your shotgun out to bring down a duck.
It's a cruel joke. The only thing to do, boys, is go ahead and
approach the blind that seems to be occupied and poke the hunters
with a stick: if they don't move, haul them in for evidence after
you bag your limit.

*   *   *   *   *   *   *   *   *   *

MINNESOTA BIGFOOT WAS SIGHTED THIS EVENING
in 1985 in a corner of the James G. Hill house in St. Paul during
a party, where a woman wearing a long gown and a mask of cosmetics walked up and said she wanted to share with him that he
seemed to be in the last stages of psychotic depression—it was
evident from his physical appearance and silence. And how could
she help him? Bigfoot assumed this was Mrs. Hill, because she
acted like she owned the place. Before he ducked out the back
door, he thought she could best help him and all the other primates
at the party by wearing less perfume and minding her own business,
whatever that was.

*   *   *   *   *   *   *   *   *   *

20

ON THIS DAY IN 1951 HAROLD MIRE, TWELVE YEARS
old, was baptized by the total-immersion method in a Baptist
church. The teenage girl who stood in the wings with him in a white
robe went first. All he could remember clearly was how he had

noticed the wet cloth clinging to her body when she walked up out
of the baptistry. He tried to keep his eyes off this beautiful, watery
creature but he could not. It was the wrong thing to do in the
circumstances: he knew it then and he knew it to this day. But
although he had lost some points for letting his earthly desires get
the best of him, he had nevertheless been saved by grace, according
to the rules. Nobody's perfect.

*   *   *   *   *   *   *   *   *   *

21

SEVENTEEN HUNDRED AND FORTY-FIVE MINNESOTANS
opened a new box of cornflakes this morning in 1985. Of this
number, whose ages ranged between seven and 103, 398 pulled
off the paper tab on top meant to fool you into thinking the box
could be reclosed. Seventeen hundred and eighteen people, including all of those who destroyed the handy closure tab and the
lady who would turn 104 tomorrow and should have known better
by then, tried to open the inner package carefully but ended up
ripping it in such a way that when the flakes were poured, a bowl
roughly two feet in diameter would have been needed if they were
to stay on target.

*   *   *   *   *   *   *   *   *   *

22

HAROLD MIRE BROUGHT HIS BIFOCALS HOME ON
this day in 1986 while Ethel was off at church sorting and packing
donated clothes for the mission field. He didn't want any witnesses
to his further decline; this would be a private moment between an
aging adult and his eyeware. Yes, he was thankful, he had told the
doctor, that the lenses didn't have the telltale horizontal line that
beautiful women could see when they walked by him, but when
Harold tried reading the newspaper for the first time, he had to
throw his head back so far he felt like a turkey drowning itself in
a rainstorm. And because his rampant nostril hair would be getting
so much extra exposure with this new reading style, he would have
to clip it every day now.

He wondered why he didn't just check all the boxes and get a
bid price on a package deal at the Medical Park while he was at

it and be done with it: artificial hip, pacemaker, hearing aid, Epsom salts, heating pad.

When Ethel got home she told Harold his new glasses made him look handsome. He could've hugged her. But why didn't he? Sometimes he was hopeless.

* * *   *   *   *   *   *   *   *

23

Your house has been selected on this day to be a display model for the new EXTRUDEL siding. We will install free of charge the top-grade EXTRUDEL-SIDE on your house and all we ask is that you allow people to drive by and look at it. What is EXTRUDEL-SIDE? It is the only siding on the American market today that is produced by the exclusive extrusion method used by the finest pasta makers. No seams, no cracks, no unsightly nails.

But what do you care, when it's free? No obligation, no hidden costs—well, one hidden cost: we can't very well haul the EXTRUDEL from Arkansas, spend three weeks at your house with a crew of hungry EXTRUDEL installation professionals, and not expect you to pay something. Let's be realistic—we want you to pay the freight on materials and provide one noon meal and a shower to the boys each day they are camped in your yard.

But what *you* get is EXTRUDEL. Once your neighbors see the beautiful new exterior of your home, they'll want it on their houses. And here's the beauty of it: for every neighbor who wises up and goes with EXTRUDEL, you get a finder's fee of $500.

Too good to be true? How can they do it? There's got to be a trick? Come on, that kind of negative thinking isn't what made America what it is today. If you don't say yes to this offer, your neighbors will beat you to the punch and you'll be sitting there with your finger up your nose in that dump with the crappy wood siding, still wondering how the world passed you by again.

* * *   *   *   *   *   *   *   *

24

ON THIS COOL FALL DAY IN 1979 THE MIRE FAMILY sat down and discussed the chicken situation in conversational tones, and even Lily, who was eight years old, agreed that:

1. The chicks they got in April were cuter than all get-out.
2. Of the twenty chickens, nineteen developed into roosters.
3. They would keep the hen for the egg.
4. All the chickens did an excellent job of eating scraps, crickets, box-elder bugs, spiders, and grain, while at the same time not pooping on the stoop as much as people said they would.
5. Roosters did not produce eggs.
6. They had a food freezer.
7. Chicken meat was human food.
8. Something had to be done.
9. They would do it the way Ethel's grandma had done it, the natural way, outdoors, with no malice and a little forethought.
10. They'd better get started.
11. Harold would sharpen the ax and get the stump ready with the two nails for holding the chicken's head. (Harold was on record as saying he hated this.)
12. Lily would be in charge of catching the chickens in the shed and bringing them over to the preparation area.
13. Ethel would start the fire in the circle of stones in the yard and put on the big tub of water for dipping the chickens so the feathers could be plucked.
14. Harold would put up a twine line between two trees for the dripping phase of the process.
15. Harold would be the man with the ax.

The assembly line was ready by midmorning and the water was boiling when Lily brought over the first rooster, holding its feet and covering its eyes with her other hand so it would be calm. She said, "This is Egbert." Harold and Ethel had forgotten that Lily had named the chickens—but then she named everything, even the big spider that lived on the porch.

"How can you tell?" Harold said.

"Egbert has a funny comb. But so does Dopey, but Dopey walks kind of sideways. He's the only one that does that."

Ethel already had a catch in her voice. "Is Dopey your favorite?"

"Oh, no, that's Lonnie the Leaper. He's a good jumper. We should save him for last."

Harold looked at Ethel and Ethel looked at Harold. "Put Egbert in the shed with the others," Harold said. "That hen needs all the company she can get."

"Edna the Elegant would like that," Lily said.

*   *   *   *   *   *   *   *   *   *

25

BY THIS DAY IN 1987 THE MINNESOTA TWINS WERE World Series champions for the first time and the Homer Hanky had been invented by the *Star-Tribune* and was a runaway bestseller. But some other Minnesota Twins homer memorabilia failed to catch on (although more valuable than the hankies if you still have them): Homer Shoestrings, Homer Duck Calls, Homer Hoops, Homer Cotton Swabs, Homer Paperweights, Homer Suppositories (for the treatment of Homer Hemorrhoids), and Homer Throat Lozenges (for treatment of Homer Voice Loss caused by yelling). The last two products were effective, but unfortunately they had very similar packaging and capsule shape.

*   *   *   *   *   *   *   *   *   *

26

THE PACKAGE ETHEL HAD ORDERED FOR HAROLD from the Mind Control Company arrived by UPS today in 1988. It was an audio tape that was supposed to help Harold learn how to relax through a combination of soft music, natural sounds, and subliminal suggestions. When Ethel came home from substitute-teaching, Harold was asleep on the couch and the relaxation tape and instruction booklet were still in the box.

"It worked," he said. "I read some of that baloney and my eyes started drooping. Maybe you should check my blood pressure, I don't think I have any. I have never been so relaxed. Whatever it cost, it was worth it. You should try it—you look kind of tense right now."

*   *   *   *   *   *   *   *   *   *

27

HAROLD RECEIVED A LETTER FROM HIS BROTHER Bill on this day in 1988. There was no greeting, no date, no inside

address. The first paragraph was a single word: "phootons." Harold
assumed he meant to write "photons," because Bill earned his living
at physics out in southern California doing something mysterious.
But the next paragraph cleared that up. He had misspelled "futon."
And he had visited their sister Carole.

*No, I don't mean [Bill wrote] the little particle with zero
mass, if that's what you were thinking. A phooton has plenty
of mass and it's thin and lumpy. I had to make a trip to Minneapolis on business, and, no, I didn't have time to come out
to your place. It's a five-hour drive—why am I telling you that?
Anyway, I get tired of the Radisson, even though the company
gives me the full ride on it. I suppose an executive suite with
a refrigerator full of snacks sounds pretty good to a guy living
in the middle of a cornfield. [It didn't.] Anyway, I'm glad Carole
moved to St. Paul—I can stay with her and it's nice to see the
kids roar around the house on their trikes. They've already got
grooves worn in the hardwood floor. And also get to know Frank
better. Actually I don't know him at all. Has he always stared
like that? [No—Bill probably brought it on.]*

*Have you guys stayed yet in that torture chamber she in-
stalled upstairs? It's got this phooton mattress that unrolls on
the floor. I asked her what would be the objection to a cot or
a sofa bed, and she said that she discovered phootons when she
was at the U. in the '70s and that it was the most natural way
in the world to sleep. I asked her how come she and Frank had
a waterbed then. And she said the doctor had told him to get
one for his back. No wonder he had a bad back if they'd been
sleeping on phootons. I asked her what it was filled with and
she said cotton. I told her it felt like granola. I said if she was
committed to the phooton concept could she at least get one for
me that was filled with toephoo?*

*The other thing is, the phooton room is the kids' playroom,
and every time you flop over to find a position where there's a
chance to fall asleep on that 100-percent-cotton slab, you crack
your head on an educational toy.*

But I'm not complaining.

Harold was glad to get another letter from Bill, even without the
signature. That put Harold's lifetime total from Bill so far at *two*.

The first one was written in 1973. That meant he could expect the third letter from Bill in 2003. But Harold wasn't complaining either.

*   *   *   *   *   *   *   *   *

28

Maybe today you should call CARL'S CANINE FURNACE SERVICE and get that forced-air heating plant of yours ready for the winter start-up. Carl does more than change the filter and thump your thermostat—he sends his trained furnace dogs (terriers, spaniels, Dobermans, or St. Bernards, depending on furnace size) through the hot- and cold-air ducts of your entire heating system, where they search out and remove the summer's accumulation of dust balls, bobby pins, socks, pizza, term papers, houseplants, mushrooms, lizards, bats, mashed potatoes, and some other things you wouldn't want to know about probably, but if you do, ask to see his list.

*   *   *   *   *   *   *   *   *

29

HAROLD'S FRIEND CHARLOTTE DROPPED BY THE place on this day in 1987 to return a salad bowl, and stayed for what would have been a chat if it had been anybody else but Charlotte, who was never interested in the weather or soybean prices or car mileage. Harold did not know too many women who were. Ethel was no exception, but Harold gave her a lot of credit for her valiant effort to act interested—as per her interpretation of the marriage vows—when he got wound up on engine seals or low-pressure systems, but he had enough sense not to give her a quiz over it later. Charlotte had taken no such vows, with Harold or anybody else.

After Harold had poured her a cup of coffee, she said, "How long do you think you have anyway?"

Harold could have played it for cheap laughs, but he decided on the medium-priced laughs instead: "I have probably shingled the house for the last time. If it doesn't hail."

Charlotte moved right on down the agenda: "Aren't there things you want to do?"

Yes, Harold thought: visit China, South America, Alaska, Russia, and a thousand other strange locales. But he hadn't even been to Washington, D.C., or Florida. Or International Falls. There were gravel roads within three miles of his place he had never set foot or tire on. He supposed he wished he could travel to every place on earth, including the rest of his county, but he couldn't and he had no serious regrets about it. He hated to admit that he was probably pretty happy and sort of content.

Harold said, "No, not the way you mean. I don't mind living, though, you understand."

Charlotte listed just a few of the items she wanted to check off before she left this vale of tears: world peace, justice for all, equality for women, the end of disease.

Harold said, "I'm glad you feel that way. Do you want another cup of coffee?" She said she didn't have time for it and Harold walked her out to the yard and stood by the driver's door as she started her old Pontiac.

"Why don't you raise the hood, Charlotte. It's missing. I'll take a quick look at it."

Two spark-plug wires had been pulled loose somehow—maybe Charlotte's cats had been climbing around in there. It was a piece of cake. Harold pushed the wires back on the plugs and it was running smooth again.

Charlotte smiled and said, "How much do I owe you, Harold?"

When Harold told Ethel about it later, Ethel said, "What did you tell her?"

Harold said, "I said making her car hit on all eight cylinders again was my small contribution to world peace—and equality for women."

"What did she say?"

"Nothing. She winked at me and drove off. If the truth were known, Ethel, she's good company, but don't ever tell her I said so. It might make her self-conscious."

* * * * * * * * * *

30

This day is sponsored by THE HOME BUYERS CLUB OF MINNESOTA, who have one word of advice: Don't get your hopes up. The following definitions are reprinted by permission from the club's *Lexicon of Househunting.*

Nice Starter Home: This means that as soon as you move in you'll have to start looking for some other place to live. A starter home is big enough for one average-size person who is away from home most of the time, or two small people who don't mind a continuous state of intimacy.

Dream Home: The owner built it in his sleep.

A Fixer-Upper: Don't turn on the lights to look at it until you wrap some tape around the bare wires. Have a priest, rabbi, or pastor present when you close on this one.

Owner Must Sell: Of course he must, because he's been renting it to five Vo-Tech students in the Auto Body program, who refinish cars in the living room when they aren't drinking beer or racing their ATV's around the house and over the porch.

Charm with Economy: The whole house is built with quarter-inch paneling and shag carpet, inside and out—except for the roof, which has a few shingles here and there, and the basement, which used to be cement blocks.

Quiet Neighborhood: Nobody else wanted to build on top of the old industrial landfill and asbestos dump.

Usable Basement: You can use it for scuba diving during the rainy season, and in the winter you can wear a parka and play Ping-Pong in a crouch.

Must See to Believe: Exactly right.

*   *   *   *   *   *   *   *   *   *

31

This day has been purchased by Carl Potsdam, CEO of AUTOMATIC SNOW RAKE, INC., in order to bring you a safety update on the Midwest's best motorized machine for removing snow from your roof. It may very well be the last roof-rake you ever have to buy. Here's Carl:

In the operating manual for the AUTOMATIC SNOW RAKE you were originally told to STAND IN FRONT OF THE MACHINE WHEN STARTING IT. *That should read* DON'T *stand in front of the machine. Otherwise it could grab you and shake you like a dog with a rat.*

Now, about the SNOW RAKE anchor rope you throw over the peak of the roof to hold the motor unit. We have found that it is best to secure this rope to a solid object like a tree or a garage, not to a car bumper, as was originally stated in the instructions. *Let's say you were on the other side of the roof adjusting the SNOW RAKE and somebody got in the car you had the rope tied to and drove off to the grocery store to get some spaghetti. Theoretically the SNOW RAKE operator could be taken for an unexpected trip. Luckily my wife looked in the rearview mirror and saw me waving my arms.*

One other slight problem. If your SNOW RAKE does not have a retainer ring on the transverse scraper cog, don't operate it until you send for the cog kit; otherwise, theoretically the SNOW RAKE could also automatically clear your roof of the shingles underneath the snow. It pulled my chimney over, too. I'm just thankful the upstairs bedroom wasn't damaged. And by the way, the retainer ring goes on the left side, not the right. That's your left as you face the SNOW RAKE from the back. Unless you bought your SNOW RAKE in Iowa. Then the retainer ring goes on the right side, not the left. That would be your right as you face the back.

Thank you for your attention.

* * * * * * * * * *

> # END OF OCTOBER

NOVEMBER

1

AFTER HAROLD AND ETHEL RETURNED HOME THIS evening in 1988 from a housewarming at the Ericksons' place, northwest of Mortwood, Harold started his post-party wrap-up for the sleepy audience of one, who was sure she would have heard much of it before, but marriage carries with it certain obligations.

"Did you use their bathroom?"

"No," Ethel said.

"Well, I visited it twice. Once to release some filtered beer, and the second time to verify that I hadn't been hallucinating."

"Interesting," Ethel said.

"A bathroom has two functions in my estimation. The first is obvious and the second is to wash all or part of your body and dry off and get out of there."

"This isn't your 'If We Lived in Caves' speech, is it?"

Harold said, "No. I have nothing against a bathroom. Simple indoor plumbing is, now that you mention it, the unnatural consequence of building a cave with two-by-fours and Sheetrock instead of finding it carved out of a hill. But it's no stranger than a drive-in bank or a twenty-four-hour supermarket."

It was getting familiar fast, so Ethel said, "What was it you didn't like about their bathroom?"

"Number one, you had to wade thirty feet from the toilet to the sink across a sea of yellow carpet that hadn't been mowed for a while. And I use the word 'sink' loosely: it was ten feet of Formica with a basin that was large enough, if it belonged to Merle Haggard it would have been shaped like a guitar. The flush handle on the polka-dot toilet was behind the tank and under it. Hidden. The sunken tub was another thirty feet north of the sink and up a steep rise to a plateau overlooking a rain forest. They've got more floor space in their bathroom than we've got in our living room, and it was cleaner."

Ethel knew what was coming next.

"If we had to start civilization all over again from scratch, the Erickson sanitary amusement park would be one of the last things that would be developed, right after automatic car-washes and breath mints."

That was his big conclusion. Ethel didn't really know for sure if she was baiting him or not when she said, "Could we have a vanity with a Formica top sometime? I'd like to have someplace besides the edge of the tub to set my stuff down."

Harold said it was fine with him. No problem. "And maybe while we're at it we could just do the whole house as a motel, with pop machines on both floors, a front desk, furniture with thin pointed legs, and a bottle opener on the bathroom door."

It was bedtime.

*   *   *   *   *   *   *   *   *   *

2 JUST BEFORE MIDNIGHT ON THIS DAY IN 1985 Minnesota Bigfoot was barely sighted through the thick smoke at the Boxelder American Legion hall playing drums in a country-western band. In the middle of "Mule Skinner Blues," the lead guitarist gave Bigfoot the nod and he went nuts on a long solo that included popping his finger out of his mouth and rapping on his head with his knuckles, but by that time the crowd was so drunk hardly anybody noticed. But the boys in the band gave him thumbs up. They had to have him back.

*   *   *   *   *   *   *   *   *   *

3 TODAY IN 1988 A SURPRISE PARTY WAS HELD AT Jerry's Plumbing in Bellton, to celebrate twenty years in the business. The carpenters, the electrician, the town's only bricklayer, all three auto mechanics, the implement dealer, the grain-elevator operator, and anybody else who had ever worked with Jerry packed themselves into the back room and jumped out when Jerry walked in. There were ham sandwiches, there was beer, but mainly there were tools. Jerry's work habits were well known: he always left his tools at the job site and forgot where they were. It took the guys a while, but they collected Jerry's tools for him from far and wide and piled them on the floor of the shop. For the first time in twenty years, Jerry had all his tools in one spot. He was choked up. He didn't know what to say. It was the happiest day of his life. And then he really did cry when they brought out a brand-new step-

ladder for him, the first one he ever owned, but he had borrowed
every ladder in town at least once.

*   *   *   *   *   *   *   *   *   *

4 THIS NEXT DAY IN 1988 JERRY THE PLUMBER WAS
called out to look at Bill Pierson's furnace. He left a pipe wrench
behind the water heater, a screwdriver on the floor, and a partial
set of sockets inside the cover of the furnace. He also dropped a
pair of tin snips in the yard on his way out. The only thing he put
back in the van was Bill Pierson's ladder, which he would haul
around for a week and then leave at the parsonage, or was it the
schoolhouse?

*   *   *   *   *   *   *   *   *   *

5 ON THIS DAY IN 1975 PURE 10W-40 HIGH-DETER-
gent engine oil was discovered by E. E. Trudel at a drilling site
his farm near Cottonwood, Minnesota. E. E. was swamped by
investors writing out checks.

*   *   *   *   *   *   *   *   *   *

6 EMPTY FIFTY-FIVE-GALLON DRUMS OF 10W-40 PENN-
zoil and a funnel were discovered by investors on this day in 1975
out behind E. E. Trudel's granary, where his old Hudson Hornet
was parked. A week later each investor received a postcard from
Acapulco: E. E. congratulated them for their willingness to take a
risk on something that on the face of it seemed too good to be true.

*   *   *   *   *   *   *   *   *   *

7

ON THIS DAY IN 1986 ALBERT DOORBIN, A LIFELONG resident of Boxelder, finished reading *Deceptive Masculinity*, where he found out about the whole sordid business of being male, including the tendency to brag and swagger and lie.

In the opening hand of the poker game this night in 1986, Albert was betting like he had a flush wired; he could see that Lars, who had him beat in sight with two pair, was about to fold, so Albert said: "I can't pretend anymore. It's all a lie. I'm blowing smoke. I got a small pair, Lars. You got me beat. I'm sorry."

Lars said, "Gee, thanks, Albert. I'm proud of my jacks and threes, but I don't take any great credit. It could've happened to anybody. I want to thank each and every one of you for being so giving. I really appreciate that you cared enough to become deeply involved in this pot." Lars never did know when enough was enough.

*   *   *   *   *   *   *   *   *   *

8

ALBERT DOORBIN FINISHED READING *MALEVOLENT Male Bonding* on this day in 1986 where he found out that not only did he have to stop telling off-color jokes, he had to stop listening as well.

At Hotshot Bowling League that night, old Hubley started telling the one about the honeymoon couple on water skis but Albert stopped him, even though it had always been one of his favorites. He said to the team: "Listen you guys, we've got to start growing as men and persons." What they replied was off-color, so Albert pretended not to listen. Nobody ever said being a new male would be easy.

*   *   *   *   *   *   *   *   *   *

9

ALBERT DOORBIN FINISHED READING *RIDICULOUS Men and Their Ridiculous Vehicles* this afternoon in 1986. That night at the American Legion wild-game feed he informed the Legionnaires at his table that he was planning to trade his four-wheel-drive supercharged 412 in for a subcompact car, because he felt he'd be a more loving person in a vehicle with a smaller engine and a Japanese name. They told him he was crazy—that was a great deer-hunting truck.

And Albert said, "Listen, boys, last week I read this book called *Male Predators,* and I'm giving up my camo coveralls, the infrared scope, the thirty-aught-six, the shotgun, the target pistol, the waders, the whole violent shebang. Make me an offer."

And the guy on his right said, "Next thing we know, Al, you're gonna tell us you're some kind of vegetarian."

And Albert said, with a mouthful of pheasant in cream, that he had a book on it if they wanted it. A guy had to draw the line somewhere.

*   *   *   *   *   *   *   *   *   *

10

HAROLD MIRE ATTENDED A HOG BARN OPEN HOUSE today in 1988 by invitation from Dean Miles, a high-school class-mate who farmed down the road and had built himself a twenty-first-century hog-production facility. It was a beauty, you couldn't deny that: 120 feet by 70 feet, room for who knows how many hogs, walls and attic insulated to R-19, propane heat, bathroom and shower for Dean, concrete liquid waste pit for the hogs, a ventilation system that was operated by computer, a kitchen area with small stove and refrigerator (for antibiotics and maybe a can of beer), a twin-size bed for when Dean had to be out there all night, and a nineteen-inch color TV in front of a La-Z-Boy.

When Harold went over to the lunch table piled high with a variety of pork products, Dean said, "What do you think of the stainless-steel trim on all the doors?"

"It's the right touch."

"It's a spendy little hog barn, but I'm the one that's got to live with it."

"You could eat off the floors anyplace," Harold said, picking up a piece of delicious smoked ham a quarter-inch thick that had fallen out of his oversized bun. "Which is more than I could say for some restaurants I've been in."

"And that's the way it's gonna stay," Dean said.

*   *   *   *   *   *   *   *   *   *

11

THE WORLD WAR II MEMORIAL HOWITZER WAS delivered on a flatcar to the Bellton depot free of charge by the Burlington Northern this Veterans Day in 1975. Casey Goshen (China, the Pacific) lifted it off with his end-loader. Doug Olson (Korea) hooked onto it with his little Allis Chalmers and pulled it into place in the Boxelder town square. The concrete slab had been poured by Joe Kosinsky (AAF navigator, B-29). The brass plaque said FOR THOSE WHO DIED IN THE SERVICE OF THEIR COUNTRY.

The howitzer had been welded and plugged, but it was clear after it had been anchored that, had it been functional, no further aiming would have been necessary for it to take off the chimney and TV antenna of a certain house on a certain street where a certain faculty member from Prairie Gate College lived.

This professor of history had stood in front of thirty veterans at the VFW hall after he got wind of the project and told them that putting a big gun there in town as a memorial was the height of absurdity. He himself was a veteran of four years of graduate school and a grueling doctoral examination, but he still should have known better. He's lucky they were such a peace-loving bunch.

*   *   *   *   *   *   *   *   *   *

12

WHEN LILY CALLED HER DAD OUT TO THE YARD this day in 1988, Harold knew what it was by the tone of her voice; deer hunters. Three pickups were parked along the road and ten men and boys in Day-Glo orange clothing were carrying shotguns across the field from two directions a mile away. It was a commando operation. Harold could see the hunters without his glasses and he figured the white-tailed deer could do the same. But if they couldn't, they could hear them. The hunters were the model of sneakiness, all right, and had obviously practiced hunching over and walking on tiptoes, but they might as well have been riding bicycles and ringing bells, Harold said. Father and daughter looked forward to deer season every year: it was one of their traditions, like watching Laurel and Hardy movies on Sunday afternoon. Slapstick was in their blood.

*   *   *   *   *   *   *   *   *   *

13

RADON GAS WAS THE SUBJECT IN THE OFFICE AT the grain elevator today in 1988 when Harold went by to pick up a gallon of cheap white paint for the chicken shed. The manager, who had to deal with the government every day, said he thought President Reagan was behind it. Everybody agreed that somebody's pockets were being lined with the money from those radon test kits. Harold said he felt like an idiot, but he had bought a kit and tested his cellar. No radon, he said.

"Yeah, join the twentieth century, Harold. I don't imagine you got any of that arsenic-treated green lumber either in that old house of yours," the manager said.

"Or the wall-board insulation they make out of cyanide," Ollie said.

"I don't even have insulation period, unless you count the rags stuffed down the wall above the medicine cabinet so the shaving cream doesn't freeze."

"Doesn't sound dangerous enough to me," the manager said. "I don't think you're trying."

"I know where you can get some asbestos tiles real cheap," Ollie said.

"Well, the fact is Ethel has been talking about building," Harold said. "And if we do, I'll try to get some radon into the new house, even if it means sending away for an aerosol can of it to spray around the rooms. We wouldn't want people to think we didn't have a modern house."

*   *   *   *   *   *   *   *   *   *

14

A FIFTY-TON BARGE OF LUTEFISK BROKE LOOSE ON this day in 1962 and sank in the Mississippi River near St. Paul. The governor called in the National Guard to prevent looting. Headache and nausea were eventually reported as far south as Davenport, Iowa. Hauling or storing more than one ton of lutefisk was made a gross misdemeanor in 1963.

* * * * * * * * * *

15

THIS IS THE LAST DAY TO APPLY FOR THE Gopher State Interpretive Dance Grant. In 1987 Terry Gultrob used his $23,000 to produce a choreographic *tour de force* featuring an introspective young man and his girlfriend fishing for walleyes during a nuclear war. The Minneapolis *Tribune* called it "a vast improvement" over the the 1986 winner's *Life of a Bill in the State Legislature.*

* * * * * * * * * *

16

IF IT'S YOUR TURN TO HAVE THE FAMILY OVER ON Thanksgiving, begin building up to it now. You will set your alarm for 3:30 A.M. on Thanksgiving Day to wedge the turkey in the oven, and by 10:30 the walls and curtains will already smell like turkey grease, and the turkey fumes will weigh heavy in the air until Christmas. You will make dressing with a twist that might be adding oysters, black olives, and pinto beans, and you will be reminded of this *faux pas* every Thanksgiving until you expire, and it will be mentioned at your funeral. People will be flopped all over the house, asleep with their mouths hanging open. There won't be room in the refrigerator for the leftovers. People will be hungry again by 6:00, and you will have just got the dishes done.

* * * * * * * * * *

17

MINNESOTA BIGFOOT WAS SIGHTED THIS AFTER-
noon in 1986 using his Cash Card to get $50 from a machine in
Roseville. His secret number was also sighted—9832—because he
didn't shield the keyboard when he typed it in. He also left his
receipt sticking out of the slot. He had a lot to learn about personal
money management.

*   *   *   *   *   *   *   *   *   *

18

THIS MORNING IN 1988 MINNESOTA NATURE WRITER
Warren Sewil decided that both sleeping and working in his six-
by-ten-foot room was not sacrifice and isolation enough to keep the
edge sharp on his creativity. His wife came home and found that
he had hired a carpenter to install a steel-barred jail door on his
room. Warren told Vera he wanted her to slip his meals under the
door on a metal tray. He was pretty sure this would open the
floodgates and let his creative juices flow.

She in turn told him that it was high time he got out and smelled
the roses and found himself a real job similar to the one she had
been paying the bills with for the past five years while he frittered
away the days writing dumb stories about animals and shrubs.

*   *   *   *   *   *   *   *   *   *

19

ON THIS DAY IN 1987, THE FOLLOWING PHONE BILL
was received by a Minnesota family that lives in a city bigger than
a breadbox but smaller than Worthington. Needless to say this
family is not served by the Walleye Phone Company, owned and
operated by Howie Humde. Howie has one basic charge, plus long
distance, which is cheap, because you can't really call that far with
Walleye yet. Most of Howie's customers get in under nine bucks
per month.

Single-party residence service ... $16.00
Long-distance calls 38.80
Multiple-phone permission fee ...   2.50
Directory Service simulated-voice
   fee 86
Interstate end-user service cost ..   13.40
County end-user service charge ..   11.34
Township end-user service fee ...   10.35
Toll-Free surcharge 7.00
911 emergency fee 18
Wire rental to state border 2.50
Telephone-assistance-plan
   surcharge 1.10
Extended-area service fee 45
Overextended surcharge 1.87
Phone pigmentation fee if not
   black or white ....   1.20 (red)
Black phone fee................   .34
Off-white phone fee 37
Cartoon-character phone fee .....   2.60 (Mickey Mouse)
Ringer service 89
Bell-clapper surcharge 96
Customer demanded LoverLine
   number lockout 11.50
Customer demanded Dial-a-
   Norwegian number lockout 12.50
Customer demanded Kiddy-Story
   number lockout 11.50
Customer demanded Hot-
   MarketTips number lockout ...   11.75
Calling-party-busy-signal genera-
   tion fee 7.93
Earth Orbit satellite toll 3.59
Incoming-call chirp charge for re-
   mote phone..................   1.75
Coffee-break kitty for regional ex-
   change staff 9.85
Supervisory personnel retirement
   fund 3.40
Smart remarks to operator 6.00

Overproduced phone-answering-
  machine message 3.20
Idle-chatter charges 3.58
Your share of "We're Your Best
  Friend" advertising-campaign
  costs during Super Bowl
  weekend 7.57
Touch-Call button service (red
  phone) 2.00
Touch-Call button service
  (Mickey Mouse). 2.50
One too many "reach out and
  touch someone" jokes 5.50
Accidental disconnection with
  chin or nose 78
Rampaging around the house and
  scaring the kids by threatening
  to tear out all the phones and
  move to a one-room cabin in
  the Yukon 10.00
Phone-bill printing fee 50
Phone-bill postage 1.08
Calling Super Valu to ask if they
  have Prince Albert in the can . .   3.00
Twisting the cord while talking . .   1.97
Slamming the phone down 3.56
Use of present service to scout
  out another company 3.70
Mutilation of last month's return-
  of-payment card 1.20
Trying to get the time of day
  from the operator (not offered)   2.56
Waiting too long to answer 3.49
Second-thought fee (hanging up
  before called party answers) . . .   1.32
Writing letter to editor in which
  you state that prior to deregula-
  tion service was better by a
  long shot and a "hell of a lot"
  cheaper 37.50

Kiddy-Story, Dial-a-Norwegian,
   LoverLine, HotMarketTips
   charges before lockout demand   896.40
SUBTOTAL:.....................   1183.53
STATE REGULATORY AGENCY MAN-
   DATED REFUND FOR ALLEGED
   PHONE COMPANY OVERCHARGES
   IN 1986.....................   .12 (credit)
TOTAL AMOUNT DUE TOMORROW: $1183.41

*   *   *   *   *   *   *   *   *   *

20

HAROLD MIRE'S UNCLE MORTON DROPPED BY TO SAY
howdy today in 1987 on his way home from buying a hundred
head of feeder calves out in Hymore, South Dakota. Mort had
been making the big trip to Hymore for cattle since the '50s, and
even when cattle stopped being such a bargain to raise and sometimes even cost money to raise, he kept it up. He was a cattleman,
plain and simple. Mort always picked a prime steer for the freezer
before he shipped the herd to market—but what he liked about
cattle was not so much the steaks and hamburger and roasts as it
was the warm companionship when he fed them on a cold winter
morning. They were peaceful creatures, he told Harold, and if they
were good for nothing except company, that would justify their
existence in his feedlot, not that he would want just anybody to
know that.

*   *   *   *   *   *   *   *   *   *

21

MINNESOTA BIGFOOT WAS SIGHTED IN A MINNEAPOLIS
appliance store this day in 1986 where he was looking hard at the
automatic dishwashers, the embodiment for him of civilized life.
He lumbered back and forth between the various models and did
quite a bit of head-scratching. It was a big decision for a hairy
primate who did not own any dishes. He kept coming back to the
Supremo, with the pot-scrubber cycle—it was a nice option in case

he ever bought some pans. He also liked his color choices with the
Supremo, which had the reversible panels, gold to silver.

*   *   *   *   *   *   *   *   *   *

22

Another day brought to you by BIGGER HAMMER HARD-
WARE—and another true story from their vault of fiascos:

☞ FRANK'S STORY

*I decided to insulate my house with one of those big blowers and
that ground-up stuff. So I drilled the first hole through the siding in
the upper story and stuck the hose nozzle in and cranked up the
blower and started pumping insulation. I put in three bags . . . four
bags. . . . I got up to thirty bags, which I thought was supposed to
be enough for the whole house, and yet it all went in one hole.
That's when my wife came running out of the house with the kids.
They were fuzzy with insulation, on their eyebrows and everywhere.
What happened was I had drilled through the wall into the upstairs
bathroom, right where the medicine cabinet was, and the insulation
pushed the door open, filled the bathroom, filled the hallway, crept
down the stairs, and was a foot deep in the living room when my
wife saw it coming toward her and escaped with the kids. I'm not
proud. I called BIGGER HAMMER and they finished the job for me
and it only cost about twice as much as it would have if I had hired
somebody to do it in the first place. But I wouldn't have learned
anything that way.*

*   *   *   *   *   *   *   *   *   *

23

HAROLD MIRE MADE SUPPER FOR ETHEL AND LILY
tonight in 1987 featuring only the favorite foods of his brothers
and sisters when they were growing up. The soup course was Campbell's tomato with double milk and a fistful of saltines: Harold's
favorite.

Harold's brother Bill was a sandwich enthusiast; his great love was peanut butter and runny grape jelly on two slices of fresh white bread. Bill liked the challenge of a leaky sandwhich when he balanced it on the back of his horizontal right hand and nibbled around it by rotating his hand 360 degrees. The trick was to eat the whole sandwich without ever gripping it or having it slide off, which Bill had down to a science by age forty. Ethel had to use her nose to adjust her sandwich, and Lily went outside and fed hers to the cats off the back of her hand. Harold did fairly well until he tried his brother's grand finale: he raised his hand above his head and then dropped it fast and almost snapped the free-falling last bite out of the air.

To clear the palate, Harold brought on his brother's Larry's two favorites (they went together): (1) a puffy hot dog boiled in water and placed in a standard hot-dog bun with some salt and (2) instant chocolate pudding, for dipping the hot dog in.

After the Larry course, Ethel and Lily said they were full, so Harold said he would cook his sisters' favorite foods for breakfast.

* * * * * * * * * *

24 HAROLD MIRE WAS UP EARLY THIS MORNING IN 1987 frying his sister Carole's beloved childhood food, floppy bacon: this was bacon cooked so that it was translucent and slick and would hang down on both sides of your fork like a noodle. Ethel and Lily both said the texture bothered them, but they did try to finish the Hostess Ho-Hos that Carole always had for breakfast with her floppy bacon.

The breakfast beverage was the cheapest instant coffee Harold could find, the only kind his sister Marie had been drinking since sixth grade. She had a metabolism that allowed her to get through the day on tap coffee, which was made by putting a teaspoon of instant coffee in the bottom of a cup and then running warm city tap water into it. Harold and Ethel's water came from a well, so Harold had made a special trip into Mortwood the day before for a gallon of chlorinated water and warmed it to eighty degrees on the stove before stirring it into the pale-brown powder in the bottom of the cup.

* * * * * * * * * *

25

MAYBE YOU'RE THINKING ABOUT GOING TO A MOVIE
tonight with your husband if you can get him off his butt, but he
could bend over at the theatre to see what that gooey stuff was
sticking his shoe to the floor and could fall over into the lap of the
lady next to him, who could scream for the manager, who could
drag him down the aisle and call the newspaper, and you could
leave your purse under the seat and it would be stolen, and by the
time you got your husband bailed out of jail, you could come home
to a burglarized house furnished with nothing worth fencing. On
the other hand, if you just stay home with the human slug you
should know that the twenty-six-inch console TV set could be de-
fective and send out X rays right toward your husband's recliner
and render him impotent. It's always a tough call to figure out what
to do with an evening.

*   *   *   *   *   *   *   *   *   *

26

This day through 1991 is sponsored by AMERICAN
FAMILY LEASING, the way to go if you already own a personal
computer, a CD player, a sailboat, a lake home, a Porsche, a
Mercedes, a condo in Florida, and you think you're ready for a
family. Check with your accountant, of course, but LEASING might
make more sense with your life-style.

Why should you tie yourself down for the long haul when you
could lease a family for a week, a month, or a year without major
emotional involvement? Maintenance is handled by AMERICAN
FAMILY LEASING. At the end of the lease agreement, you do have
the option of purchasing the family. Or you may wish to trade it in
for a new model, as most of our customers do.

Leasing from AMERICAN FAMILY will allow you to participate
in the social institution that made our country great, but without
the time-consuming attachments that so often develop in the tra-
ditional family units.

*   *   *   *   *   *   *   *   *   *

27

ON THIS DAY IN 1988 A TWIN CITIES NEWSPAPER announced that the crime rate in Furman, Minnesota, had jumped 400 percent in 1987. Concerned citizens pounced on the town council and asked them to get immediate preliminary bids on a law-enforcement center and jail complex similar to the facility down the road in the county seat that had a bulletproof command center and beautiful landscaping.

* * *   *   * *   *   * * *

28

THE REPORT FROM THE BUREAU OF CRIME STATISTICS arrived at the mayor's office in Furman today; he called another council meeting to announce the following information:

1. In 1986 only one crime had been reported in Furman— Donny Drewson had made an illegal U-turn and raced his engine and had been issued a ticket by Deputy Tom Timmerson. Tom had checked "Terroristic Threats" on the state form as best describing Donny's crime.
2. In 1987 Tom had reported four crimes to the Bureau:
   a. Sarah Mitter had failed to observe the no-smoking sign at the Senior Center in March.
   b. Bob Moline was cited for sitting in a lawn chair in his front yard in full public view sipping a can of beer.
   c. An out-of-state male was booked for putting leaded gasoline in his car at the Texaco station after modifying the filler pipe.
   d. An unnamed juvenile had been handcuffed and taken home after purchasing an ice-cream bar in Orv's Market wearing no shirt and no shoes.

In view of these new facts, the council voted to cancel the plans for the law-enforcement center and leave Tom's office where it was, in the back of the laundromat, and he could continue to give change for the machines and the soap dispensers when he wasn't busy with criminal investigations. While they were at it, the council decided what to do about the sewage lagoon when the wind was from the east: nothing.

*   *   *   *   *   *   *   *   *   *

29

TODAY IN 1985 WHICH HAPPENED TO BE A FRIDAY, Harold Mire finished reading a ghostwritten book about a guy who had been wounded and oppressed by his fundamentalist parents and was spending the rest of his life getting over it. The book was darn funny, but if you thought about it, it was sad, too. That's the way Harold read it, anyway, but he wasn't a literary critic. As a consequence of losing himself in the book, Harold launched into a semi-vigorous self-examination of his own upbringing.

He looked at the role his parents' religious beliefs had played in his upbringing. Had they forced him to go to church when he didn't want to go, for instance? "No" would have to be the answer. To this day, like his father, Harold could take it or leave it. He saw no problem whatsoever in going to church—or not going to church, which was his tendency, even though Ethel and Lily were regulars.

Every once in a while Harold would suit up and get a big boost out of seeing some of his friends and neighbors in a situation that seemed to say there was something essentially decent and wonderful about human beings. Harold always had the urge to go to church more often after that, since it was pleasurable. But what if he got in the habit of going? He wasn't ready to take the chance. But he didn't feel guilty about it one way or the other—he guessed he had his parents to thank for that.

*   *   *   *   *   *   *   *   *   *

30

HAROLD WAS OUT IN THE YARD SPLITTING WOOD with the Monster Maul this Saturday afternoon in 1985 thinking about the book he had finished yesterday, still trying to find some permanent damage inflicted on him by his parents.

Could it be those family get-togethers?

It was a rare Sunday in the late '40s when the whole family didn't pile in the '42 Plymouth about 11:00 in the morning and drive fifty miles north to the Fremson area, where his dad's people lived on farms, the purpose of the trip being to eat a big dinner and hang around with people you liked who happened to be your relatives. It was an extended family—it extended from the house all the way out to the yard where the cars were parked. When dinner was over, the women washed the dishes and put away the perishables for supper, and the men drifted out to the yard in a loose herd, following the Biblical precedent set in the Revised Detroit Version: "On the seventh day you should talk cars."

Harold had three choices in those days: either stay in the house and risk being asked to dry dishes, or hide and leaf through stacks of *Farm Journals*, or go out and stand around with the men as they looked under the hood of something and discussed the linkage in the column shifter, say, or the odd engine mounts. It didn't much matter what it was, Harold didn't think it looked odd or funny or even too interesting in those days.

What he had appreciated was the joking. The Mire clan wasn't big on practical jokes and they never *told* jokes much either, as in "Did you hear the one about the sick Hereford and the vacuum-cleaner salesman?" Their joking was embedded in the talk, and even though Harold did not understand the details as a boy, he laughed at the delivery. The Mires were also kidders—they loved to give you a hard time, especially if you had made a poor decision with your last car, had really got yourself a woofer.

Cars. Could Harold blame his parents for his obsession with cars and his tendency to talk about them too much? It went deep, no doubt about it, but in his opinion it was harmless. But maybe he was kidding himself.

*   *   *   *   *   *   *   *   *   *

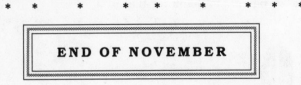

END OF NOVEMBER

DECEMBER

1 This day brought to you by UNCLE BARNEY'S DRIED BACHELOR DINNERS, the simple freeze-dried meal in a box you tear open and pour into a pan, add water, and boil on a hotplate until the hard chunks get soft. And you can eat it right out of the pan when it's done. The Uncle Barney philosophy is that a guy living alone doesn't need candlelight and china. You just come home, boil yourself up an UNCLE BARNEY'S DRIED BACHELOR DINNER, plop down on the couch and watch the evening news in your skivvies, and try not to get your head stuck in the pan.

Try Uncle Barney's original recipe, Sliced Turkey Wieners & Mashed Potatoes with Corn, or one of these new taste treats: Calf Liver and Sauerkraut, Rice O'Baloney, Ketchup & Beans, Sardines with Dills, or Floating Shepherd Pie. One box, one pan: life doesn't get any easier. Look for Uncle Barney's dinner in the bachelor section of your supermarket. A word of caution: never try to save more time by eating Uncle Barney's dinners *dry* or you could develop a serious case of cramping bloat.

* * * * * * * * * *

2 ON THIS DAY IN 1958 GANDY OLSON OF WINGERTON, Minnesota, unveiled his Suntan Bed, a machine that looked like a hog roaster with purple lights and required a person to climb inside it nude in order to get an attractive brown skin. The press was merciless, calling Olson a misguided lunatic for thinking that the American public would ever go for such a ridiculous contraption. The demoralized Gandy dumped his roaster in the Mississippi River, tore up his patent application, moved to a trailer park in Georgia and began his life as a pecan grader.

* * * * * * * * * *

3

IT WAS ON THIS DAY IN 1986 THAT THE DEBUT ISSUE
of *The Understater* began exclusive serial publication of "Confessions of a Minnesota Humorist." The name of the humorist was
never revealed and nobody was interested enough to ask. He is
clearly male, which narrows it down some. The newspaper folded
at the conclusion of the series. The "Confessions" are reprinted
here without permission because the editor was nowhere to be
found.

☞"CONFESSIONS OF A HUMORIST," PART ONE

*The sort of people who wink a lot in casual conversation think
anecdotes in sermons are meant to be funny and bear repeating.
They also tend to be tickled no end by the silly antics of their
pets, which they generally have plenty of and don't mind talking
about. It just cracks them up when their dog Bud wears Dad's
hat and barks at the television set. Listen, last fall my cat Gurgles tragically tangled herself in the box springs of my bed,
chasing a mouse probably, or maybe just horsing around. Silly,
but hardly funny. Gurgles is now resting in my backyard in a
queen-size grave.*

   *   *   *   *   *   *   *   *   *

"CONFESSIONS OF A HUMORIST" CONTINUED ON THIS
day in 1986:

*If a humorist has a wife who will stay with him, people say this
to her all the time: "It must be fun living with such a funny
guy, a riot." This makes her laugh, maybe for the first time in
weeks.*

    *Some people imagine that a humorist chuckles to himself
all day and even wakes up in the night to do it. When he is in
front of a typewriter, though, they figure he is totally out of*

control. *Periodically something he writes is so hilarious he bounces up and down in his chair, slapping his thighs and bellowing. The glasses come off, the hanky comes out. Pretty soon he is on the floor, kicking his heels and gasping for breath.*

For your information, the average humorist is never rendered senseless by his own wit, or anybody else's, either. He spends his days in a smoky room, with the shades pulled and the door closed. What he does in there is his business. Three or four times a week he makes a loud noise that can be heard through the door, but nobody would ever take it for a guffaw or a chuckle.

In the popular lay mind, being humorous is confused with being happy. The humorist never makes that mistake. His job is writing humor. There's no law that says he has to enjoy himself. And even if there was he wouldn't.

*   *   *   *   *   *   *   *   *   *

 TO EVER-DECLINING READERSHIP "CONFESSIONS OF a Humorist" continued on this day in 1986:

How many old and wise humorists do you know? For that matter, how many young and wise ones do you know? It is every humorist's dream to be a serious writer—for health's sake, if nothing else—which is why several months ago I thought I'd try to get out more and be less comic and maybe stop smoking and drinking so much.

I invited myself—because they would never have thought of it—to a Sunday brunch at the Flowering Muse, which is a New Age watering hole for writers who deal exclusively with tough issues and powerful emotions. As long as I'm confessing, I will say that the croissants were good and the fruit bar had a great selection of exotics. But when I tried to send this idea I had up the flagpole about two guys in a barren landscape crushed by remorse and guilt, because I didn't know where to go with it, they were all busy telling Norwegian jokes and knocking over their water glasses. Finally one of the men—whose claim to fame is a cycle of very serious stories on intestinal diseases—said, "Why don't you lighten up or else take a hike?"

You don't have to tell me something twice. It was back to
the dark room.

*   *   *   *   *   *   *   *   *   *

6

THE LETTERS TO THE EDITOR WERE LONGER THAN
today's excerpt from "Confessions of a Humorist" in 1986:

The world is predominantly non-humorous, mostly because of
the way life is structured: You are born and after that you die.
In between you suffer. The humorist never sends to ask for
whom the bell tolls: he wasn't born yesterday.

My Cousin Eddie (his real name) doesn't send to ask either;
he uses the telephone to get the information fresh. "Ed here,
big fellow. I heard the bells tolling this morning. Who was it
this time?" Eddie's favorite saying when he's having fun, which
is most of the time, is "Make hay while the sun shines, we're
gonna be dead a long time." Then he laughs. But he's a software
designer not a humorist.

Being dead a long time is not a humorous concept to me.
In my opinion, death is the most counterproductive element in
the humor trade. In order to write humor I have to forget death.
I can forget to change my socks for days and keep pulling the
same dirty pair out from under the bed, but forgetting Mr.
Death? Forget it.

*   *   *   *   *   *   *   *   *   *

7

THE SERIAL PUBLICATION OF "CONFESSIONS OF A
Humorist" mercifully concluded on this day in 1986:

Humorists are rarely invited to parties. Myself, I don't have
parties, but if I did I wouldn't invite humorists either. Not being
invited to parties suits me fine, because some well-meaning
person in the party mood will always come over to me and say,
"Oh what a wonderful time you must have. Everything is funny,

isn't it? Fireplugs, garbage trucks, people at Burger World, pencil erasers. Everything!!!" The old story.

I have news for you. Everything is not funny. Hardly anything is funny. A guy has to make things funny. Making pencil erasers funny could take a while—you could die doing it.

Not that I mean to encourage you, but I was asked to say a few clear words about how to get started in the lucrative field of humor writing: It's simple. First you forget you-know-what (here's a hint: it rhymes with "bad breath") and then you direct your attention to the garbage truck parked behind Burger World. Right away you notice that the driver's head is shaped like a fireplug smoking a cigarette. If you keep working at it, pretty soon it could even be humorous.

A humorous garbage truck may seem to you like mighty little consolation in a world of overwhelming mortality, but sometimes it's all we have. That's what I think is funny.

*   *   *   *   *   *   *   *   *   *

8 ON THIS COLD NIGHT IN 1983 HAROLD MIRE WENT to bed with his radio tuned to WNAX, a country-western station out of Yankton, South Dakota, which was broadcasting the playoff games in the girls' high-school state basketball tournament. He did not follow South Dakota girls' basketball; the Minnesota girls were hard enough to follow. But it was peaceful lying in bed under four blankets in a cold farmhouse room in western Minnesota, listening to the play-by-play of basketball games when the temperature outside the window was ten below zero. In a general way he did care who won or lost, but in a specific way he didn't. He drifted off to sleep in the middle of a fast break and partisan shouting.

*   *   *   *   *   *   *   *   *   *

9 HAROLD MIRE WOKE UP AT 2:00 A.M. ON THIS DAY in 1983. He rarely slept more than three hours at a time, unless he was in a clothing store waiting for Ethel, he said. But it was nothing to worry about: he liked waking up in the middle of the night; it gave him the chance to listen to the radio. It did cross his mind occasionally that maybe he wasn't ambitious enough and probably by now he should have a portfolio of stocks and bonds and real estate. What he had instead was one-fourth of a college degree and a portable radio. Maybe listening to the radio in the night was his part in the big scheme of things.

What Harold heard was insect-like static and ghostly voices coming from his radio. WNAX was off the air. Something was wrong. He went back to sleep and woke up again about 5:00 A.M. to find WNAX back on the air. The insects were gone, but the announcer seemed to be speaking from the bottom of a barrel. He said they were experiencing a little difficulty, which Harold could have told him, but it was worse than the cheesy echo: the three-story WNAX studio building in Yankton had caught fire around midnight. It was still burning, the announcer said, but no one had been injured. They were broadcasting from the transmitter site outside of town. The weather-and-farm-news guy came on and said, "You'll have to bear witness." Harold was sure he meant to say "bear with us." Harold decided to do both.

The way it sounded to Harold, the makeshift facilities came to a grand total of one tiny room with a thirty-pound antique microphone and a child's hi-fi set for spinning the two albums somebody had brought from home: Hank Williams, Jr., and Bing Crosby, it had sounded like to Harold. He didn't catch the name.

As the two morning announcers carried on, other announcers from later shifts would drop by to give emotional accounts of the fire and to say a few sad words about what had been lost. The old building was gone, that much was clear; and with it the record library, the commercials, all the broadcast equipment not at the transmitter site or the girls' tournament, and the personal artifacts of the staff. The broadcast schedule was thrown to the wind. The biggest regional news story that day was their own fire. The announcers had their hearts on their sleeves and so did Harold.

Every so often Harold could hear what was surely a coffee cup being set down on the table next to the microphone or a beer bottle—who would deny them that? He thought he heard the squawk of an old swivel chair, and footsteps, and a door being opened. It was the old days of radio coming around again by a miracle. Harold and Ethel both bore witness—they threw their schedule to the wind, too, which wasn't all that tight to begin with.

Harold expected "Captain Midnight" to come sailing through
the ether. Or "Fibber McGee & Molly." Or maybe President Roo-
sevelt would have a little fireside chat. Maybe Harold would walk
through town tomorrow and there wouldn't be any TV sets. But
he supposed that was too much to hope for. By one o'clock that
afternoon WNAX had resumed broadcasting girls' basketball. The
fans hadn't missed one play. And that night Harold went to sleep
again with basketball coming out of the speaker of his radio.

*   *   *   *   *   *   *   *   *

10

AT 3:15 A.M. ON THIS DAY IN 1983 HAROLD MIRE
woke up to his favorite WNAX feature in the night, the state-by-
state regional weather report given always at fifteen minutes past
the hour every hour for Iowa, Minnesota, North Dakota, Nebraska,
Wyoming, Montana (east of the Continental Divide), and South
Dakota. This litany of predictions and conditions never failed to
cheer him up and make him sleepy at the same time. Like girls'
high-school basketball, the seven-state weather in the middle of
the night was a sign that couldn't be ignored: it pointed to the
kindness and nobility and grace of human beings. Harold took it
as a blessing, even if he did fall asleep in the middle of it.

*   *   *   *   *   *   *   *   *

11

ON THIS DAY IN 1961 JOHN ROHM PUT THE
finishing touches on what became known to the neighborhood in
Clayburgh as the schoolhouse. When Clayburgh's high-school
building was vacated in 1959, John got the high bid on the gym,
which he brought home with considerable effort, brick by brick
and board by board. His new house was then constructed *in toto*
from the salvaged materials. He even had a shower from the locker
room.

What bumped John from the novice eccentric class up to the
genius class was the hardwood gym floor that covered all the floors
in his house. In his half-court living room and dining room he had

installed the works, with the original paint: free-throw circles, lane, out of bounds. The basket and bang board were at the north end of the court, where John had the vaulted ceiling.

In the early '40s, John had been voted onto the all-state team four times at Clayburgh. He and Paula (all-state '46) had raised five kids in that house and every one of them had played a mean game of basketball. John himself, at sixty-five, could still stand at the free-throw line in front of the sofa and drop them in one after the other without hitting the rim or the stained-glass window. Sometimes he and Paula would play one-on-one in their sock feet.

*   *   *   *   *   *   *   *   *   *

12

TODAY IN 1987 IN THE MAIL HAROLD MIRE received a card from Bob's B-17 Park. Bob wondered why Harold hadn't been over for a while and invited him to sip some eggnog on the 15th. He said he had two engines running on the old Fortress now. The Fortress was the B-17 he had hauled up from Phoenix a few years back. It sat on the hill overlooking Bob's lake.

*   *   *   *   *   *   *   *   *   *

13

HAROLD MIRE'S CATS WERE HANGING AROUND THE kitchen window this cold morning in 1987 and staring up at him and meowing because they wanted to come inside and live in the house instead of on the hay pile or under the red shed. It was a nice try, but Harold knew that in no time he would be feeding them in the kitchen out of little cans of expensive moist chunks that made him gasp when they were opened in a closed space. The generic crunchies were plenty good if supplemented with fresh rabbit and sparrow. And besides that the drapes would be covered with hair and they would want to sleep on the bed. It was the domino theory.

*   *   *   *   *   *   *   *   *   *

14

The following heartwarming Christmas memory comes to you today courtesy of THE HANDYPERSONS' INSTITUTE:

Howdy. I'm Bjorn Hansen, handyman. When I hear the word "tool" it takes me back to the days of my youth, when I received the first tool I could call my own for Christmas, a pair of needle-nosed pliers. I was all of four years old and I remember using the pliers to straighten some of the bent struts on my erector set. Screw-drivers the next year, and before I knew it I was a teenager with Allen wrenches, wire cutters, sockets, and a complete set of open-end and box-end wrenches in all the popular sizes. And I had this wonderful green toolbox with a hip roof—a confirmation gift—and a lock that made a snapping noise. I still have that toolbox but now it's jammed full of everything I need to keep things humming around the house and in the yard. And this Christmas there'll be something I'll have to fix as soon as it comes out of the box. Can I make a suggestion? Give the gift that never needs fixing: buy a tool for somebody you love this blessed season.

*   *   *   *   *   *   *   *   *   *

15

IT WAS SNOWING PRETTY HARD WHEN HAROLD pulled into the long lane leading up to Bob's B-17 Park. Bob had strung Christmas lights on his B-17. It was a beautiful sight. In some ways Harold felt ashamed of himself that a war machine like that four-engine Fortress with turret guns should give him such a strong dose of Christmas spirit. It didn't make any sense, but then it did, too. Harold and Bob drank a little eggnog and talked a little politics. About nine o'clock a vanload of high-school kids from St. Luke's drove in and began singing Christmas carols. When they finished, Bob invited them into the B-17, passed out some cookies, and fired up the right and left outboard engines for all of them. It was quite the deal, no doubt about it. "Unmatched," Harold told Ethel and Lily when he returned home that night. "It was like going forty-five years into the past. That Bob puts on a good show when he has his heart in it."

   *   *   *   *   *   *   *   *   *

16

ON THIS EVENING IN 1986 MINNESOTA BIGFOOT WAS sighted getting to his feet and standing throughout the "Hallelujah Chorus" of Handel's *Messiah*.

   *   *   *   *   *   *   *   *   *

17

AT BREAKFAST TODAY IN 1988 ETHEL MIRE addressed the window: "We have to do something. Soon."

Harold was the only other person in the kitchen, so he replied. "Do what?"

"I don't want to grow old in this ramshackle house."

"Ramshackle" he'd heard before. "I'll need twenty-four hours to consider the full impact of your statement," Harold said. He didn't say it, but this was more surprising than the time Ethel went to Toronto by herself and never said why.

Breakfast was the Seminar Hour at the Mire home. That was enough new business for today.

   *   *   *   *   *   *   *   *   *

18

AT BREAKFAST TODAY IN 1988 ETHEL PUT OLD business from yesterday on the table immediately. She had several indictments of the present dwelling:

"The painted wallpaper on the kitchen ceiling is peeling and falling into the food. The floor is spongy, the rusty cabinets slope down to the center of the room. Nothing is sitting level, not the refrigerator, not the stove."

Harold said, "Some wood shims under the front feet would fix that."

"The ceiling?"

Harold said, "Okay, I give. I'd be the first one to agree that the kitchen could use a little work."

* * * * * * * * * *

19

ETHEL TOOK THE FLOOR THIS MORNING IN 1988 because Harold didn't. He was running scared.

"That so-called furnace in the floor of the living room. I want a furnace that I don't have to light by getting down on my hands and knees and dropping a piece of burning toilet paper into it through an open lid and hoping the oil smoke doesn't puff up."

Harold said, "You can use newspaper or Kleenex."

This seemed to be the wrong answer.

* * * * * * * * * *

20

AT BREAKFAST TODAY IN 1988 ETHEL SAID: "WHAT about that unpainted board nailed over the hole in the ceiling where you stepped through ten years ago trying to find the squirrel?"

"What do you mean, 'try'? It was dead, but I found it." Harold could feel the winds of change blowing toward him. "This is the kind of place they advertise as having rustic charm. Up in the Twin Cities people would be falling all over themselves lining up to take this house off our hands. We're talking *soul*."

Ethel was talking crowbar and dumptruck.

* * * * * * * * * *

21

HAROLD WAS HOPING ETHEL HAD CHANGED HER tune when he walked into the kitchen this morning in 1988.

"I guess I'm tired of dealing with crickets and spiders and box-elder bugs."

"It's what they call an ecosystem," Harold said. "The spiders are there to eat the crickets."

"What are we here for?" Ethel said.

* * * * * * * * * *

22

HAROLD MIRE TOOK THE FLOOR FIRST AT BREAKFAST today in 1988 and hauled out his big guns.

"This house is paid for. If another Great Depression hit, we could get by. No problem."

"It won't work, Harold. Either we fix up this house or . . ."

"Or what?"

"Or we build a new house," Ethel said.

"I've got it," Harold said. "Why don't you and Lily build a new house without crickets out by the garden and I'll stay here in the old one. We can commute the fifty yards. The walk would help keep us limber in our old age."

* * * * * * * * * *

23

"WELL?" WAS ALL ETHEL SAID THIS MORNING IN 1988.

Harold said: "I guess I could go along with building a new house in a few years, but I'd want it to look exactly like the old one."

"Exactly?"

"Maybe slightly bigger. And a real basement would be nice. The cellar is beginning to bother me, if the truth were known. In ten years or so I might not be able to creep on my belly into that crawl space under the bathroom to fix the pipes. What if I got sick under there? You'd have to tie ropes onto my feet and drag me out face down in the dirt. I couldn't put you through something like that."

There'd be more dramatics, Ethel knew that, but it was, nevertheless, checkmate.

* * * * * * * * * *

24

ON THIS CHRISTMAS EVE IN 1987 MINNESOTA Bigfoot was sighted playing a Wise Man in the Christmas program at a Lutheran church near Stony Run, Minnesota. His job was to point at the silver star in the sky and then bow down before the Peterson child wrapped in swaddling Pampers and a Pooh blanket from Sears.

*   *   *   *   *   *   *   *   *   *

25

OKAY, MERRY CHRISTMAS. BUT A FEW FRIENDLY words of advice: Get the wrapping paper and boxes cleaned up and out to the trash burner by 10:00 A.M. Take down the Christmas tree and put the decorations in the shoebox. Stop eating fudge.

*   *   *   *   *   *   *   *   *   *

26

MINNESOTA BIGFOOT WAS SIGHTED THIS DAY IN 1987 at the Mortwood Mall-Mart with a cart full of toys based on TV cartoon characters. He had some late shopping to do and the prices were right.

*   *   *   *   *   *   *   *   *   *

27

This day brought to you by FITZELSTEIN MINERAL WATER of Shallmar, Minnesota's leading bottler of liquids from the tap. Ask for a FITZIE MINNIE the next time you drop in at your favorite watering hole. Fitzelstein is available in Original Chlorinated, Lite Chlorinated, Semi-Lite, Extra-Lite with Lime, Semi-Dark with Lite Lime, Dim-Lite, Low-Salt, Dark, Dark-Lite, Low-Salt Lite, Dark Lemon, Lite Lemon Export, Domestic Lemon, Murky, and Lime-Lite.

*   *   *   *   *   *   *   *   *   *

28

HAROLD'S SISTER CAROLE CALLED TODAY IN 1988 to tell him that she had heard from Marie that he had been made

president of a bank in Minneapolis. Marie said that Bill had told
her that Mom had called Larry and Larry had called him. Carole
told Harold that anything was possible, but that she couldn't see
how a guy who spent his days repairing used machinery would
have the expertise to be president of a bank.

"Give me some credit. What would it take?" Harold said. "A
new suit and a half-acre desk, and a haircut once a week instead
of every three or four months."

Carole said that since the family communicated mostly by
phone and there was no family newsletter, something had to be
done in the area of message transmission. Maybe they could get
their brother Larry to invent a family decoder and filter they could
attach to their phones.

Harold told Carole that what he had told their mother originally
was that the bank where he had his checking account had said he
was overdrawn by $17, but it was their mistake, so the president
of the local bank had his secretary call Harold to apologize and
send him a thermal blanket they normally only give away with a
$2,000 deposit.

Carole said: "Thermo what? 'Nuclear' did you say?"

*   *   *   *   *   *   *   *   *   *

29
NOBODY MUCH NOTICED MINNESOTA BIGFOOT
driving a cab in Minneapolis on this day in 1987, except the two
New York City businessmen he picked up at the airport. They
double-tipped him and said his quiet politeness and good grooming
were refreshing.

*   *   *   *   *   *   *   *   *   *

30
ON THIS BEAUTIFUL WINTER DAY IN 1987 MAIDA
Stellman of Mortwood turned ninety years old. She still mowed
her own half-acre lawn, she washed her own storms and put them
up in the fall, she pitched tough horseshoes against her adult grand-
children, and in general felt like a young woman of seventy. She
had never had an auto accident, not even during the forty years

she drove a school bus, which she had retired from in 1963. She threw away her bifocals in 1986 after electing to have some fancy laser surgery and had twenty-twenty vision again.

But she was worried that maybe she was slipping and didn't know it. She had read plenty of stuff in the magazines about that kind of thing. Her kids, who were all retired themselves now, said, "Oh, Mom." But they might be just humoring her. So she had made an appointment to meet with a psychologist on her birthday, which was when her driver's license needed to be renewed.

She got right to it: "I'm ninety years old. I came in here to have you tell me if I'm crazy and if it's safe to have me on the road and if it's time for me to be on some sort of medication—everybody else I know is."

The psychologist—a man who had turned fifty the year before and was still depressed about it—also got right to it: "If you'll tell me how you managed to get to be ninety and still have more energy than I do, I'll pay *you* the $50 and buy you lunch besides."

"Deal," Maida said, and she drove. The psychologist felt more secure than he had for years.

* * * * * * * * * *

31

ON THIS NEW YEAR'S EVE IN 1987 HAROLD AND Ethel invited us over to see the New Year in. We drop by without calling ahead all the time, which is the way it's done where we live, but the formal invitation ("So do you want to come over then?") was a nice surprise.

Here's what we did: we drank cider, we had all the pineapple/cream-cheese bars we could eat, and we put a jigsaw puzzle together on the big round kitchen table.

The finished puzzle was thirty-two inches by twenty and the picture was an aerial photograph of Harold's five acres taken the previous August by a company that flew around doing that for a living. You could see everything, even the outhouse under the tree, and the horse, and the scarecrow in the garden dressed in feed cap and ragged chore jacket, and the '70 Chrysler, the Northern Spy apple tree, and the compost heap.

Then Harold brought out the magnifying glass so we could get a close look at the people standing in the yard by the lilac bushes.

We didn't remember the plane flying over that day. But it was us, all right, his family and mine, six of us.

Harold presented us with a framed copy of the aerial photo and then he said, "Ethel and Lily and I just want you to know that this is our place and we're never moving from here and you guys are always welcome."

Then we toasted the New Year with hot chocolate and wished each other many more days of one thing and another—and unless worse came to worst, we would do it together.

*　　*　　*　　　*　　　*　　*　　　*　　　*　　*　　*

END OF DECEMBER

FOR THE BEST IN PAPERBACKS, LOOK FOR THE

In every corner of the world, on every subject under the sun, Penguin represents quality and variety—the very best in publishing today.

For complete information about books available from Penguin—including Pelicans, Puffins, Peregrines, and Penguin Classics—and how to order them, write to us at the appropriate address below. Please note that for copyright reasons the selection of books varies from country to country.

In the United Kingdom: For a complete list of books available from Penguin in the U.K., please write to *Dept E.P., Penguin Books Ltd, Harmondsworth, Middlesex, UB7 0DA.*

In the United States: For a complete list of books available from Penguin in the U.S., please write to *Dept BA, Penguin, Box 120, Bergenfield, New Jersey 07621-0120.*

In Canada: For a complete list of books available from Penguin in Canada, please write to *Penguin Books Ltd, 2801 John Street, Markham, Ontario L3R 1B4.*

In Australia: For a complete list of books available from Penguin in Australia, please write to the *Marketing Department, Penguin Books Ltd, P.O. Box 257, Ringwood, Victoria 3134.*

In New Zealand: For a complete list of books available from Penguin in New Zealand, please write to the *Marketing Department, Penguin Books (NZ) Ltd, Private Bag, Takapuna, Auckland 9.*

In India: For a complete list of books available from Penguin, please write to *Penguin Overseas Ltd, 706 Eros Apartments, 56 Nehru Place, New Delhi, 110019.*

In Holland: For a complete list of books available from Penguin in Holland, please write to *Penguin Books Nederland B.V., Postbus 195, NL-1380AD Weesp, Netherlands.*

In Germany: For a complete list of books available from Penguin, please write to *Penguin Books Ltd, Friedrichstrasse 10-12, D-6000 Frankfurt Main I, Federal Republic of Germany.*

In Spain: For a complete list of books available from Penguin in Spain, please write to *Longman, Penguin España, Calle San Nicolas 15, E-28013 Madrid, Spain.*

In Japan: For a complete list of books available from Penguin in Japan, please write to *Longman Penguin Japan Co Ltd, Yamaguchi Building, 2-12-9 Kanda Jimbocho, Chiyoda-Ku, Tokyo 101, Japan.*

FOR THE BEST IN HUMOR, LOOK FOR THE (P)